MATTERHORN
MOUNTAIN SUMMER MEMOIR

by

VIRGINIA MAY

BAYEUX ARTS
DIGITAL-TRADITIONAL PUBLISHING

Published March 2015

Published by
Bayeux Arts Digital Traditional Publishing
119 Stratton Crescent, SW
Calgary, Canada T3H 1T7

www.bayeux.com

Cover Design: Chris Malmkvist
Book Design: Lumina Datamatics

Library and Archives Canada Cataloguing in Publication

May, Virginia, 1943-, author
    Matterhorn : Mountain Summer Memoir / Virginia May.

Issued in print and electronic formats.
ISBN 978-1-897411-83-4 (pbk.).   ISBN 978-1-897411-97-1 (ebook)

    1. May, Virginia, 1943-. 2. Mountain resorts—Matterhorn (Switzerland and
Italy)—Employees—Biography. I. Title.

TX910.5.M29A3 2015   913.494'7062092   C2015-901183-3   C2015-901294-5

The Publisher acknowledges the financial support of the Government of Canada through the Canada Book Fund, the Alberta Media Fund, and the Canada Council for its publishing activities.

Printed in Canada

Dedication

To my mum, Barbara Bartlett, who came to Schwarzsee and Zermatt that first summer and many times in the years that followed.

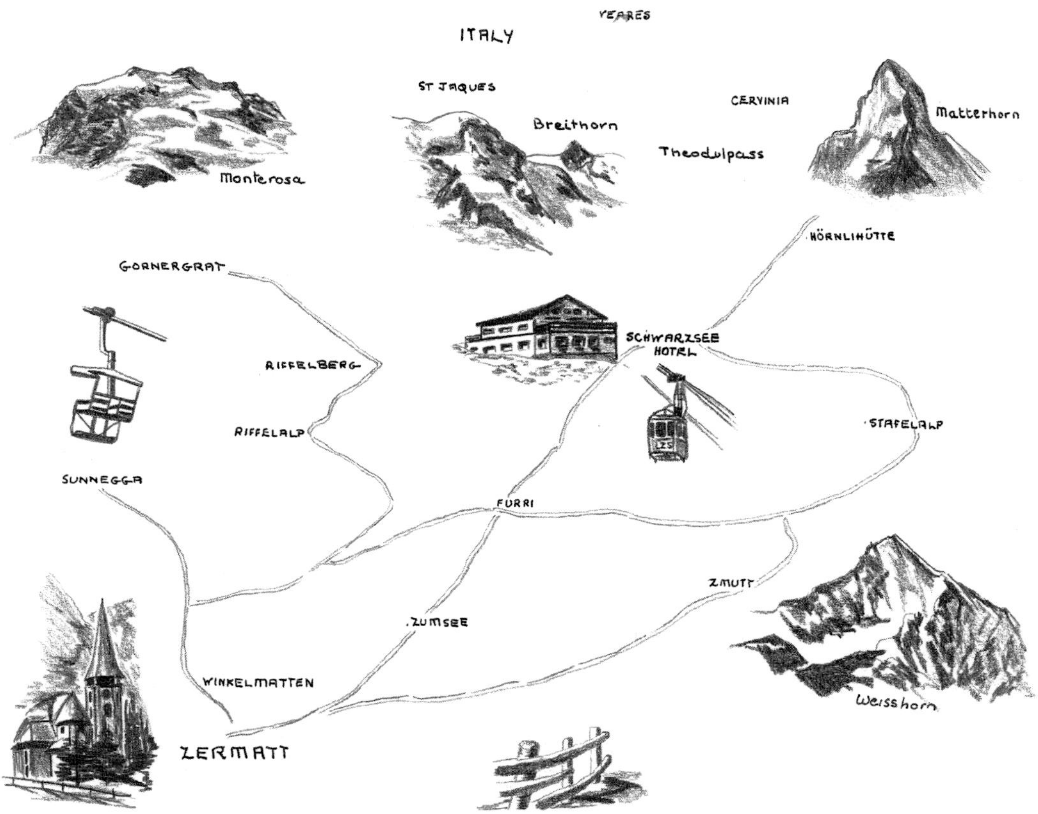

ITALY

YEARES

St JAQUES

Breithorn

CERVINIA

Theodulpass

Matterhorn

Monterosa

HÖRNLIHÜTTE

GORNERGRAT

SCHWARZSEE
HOTEL

RIFFELBERG

RIFFELALP

STAFELALP

SUNNEGGA

FURRI

Zmutt

ZUMSEE

Weisshorn

WINKELMATTEN

ZERMATT

TABLE OF CONTENTS

The paintings and black and white sketches found throughout this book are the work of Virginia May. The photographs are black and white sixties taken in the summer of 1962.

ACKNOWLEDGEMENTS

I wish to acknowledge those people who have helped me bring this long project to completion.

First is my wonderful publisher Ashis Gupta of Bayeux Arts Inc, in Calgary. He had enough faith to publish this book. Then there are Karol and Barb Fodor of Digital Arts in Calgary who helped me reproduce all my artwork in a quality suitable for publication. My son Max, an ad copywriter in Vancouver helped me edit the final text and found a wonderful freelance editor Lianne Seykora to professionally edit the text. Then I must mention my friend and past legal secretary Jeannine Reeves who took my first, very poorly typed, text and turned it into a thing of beauty that could actually be read.

I particularly want to acknowledge Chris Malmkvist who created and designed the beautiful cover for the book. Chris is a well-known eclectic artist in British Columbia, Western Canada. He came to Canada from Sweden in the 50's and has became famous for his soapstone sculptures, acrylics, oils and etchings.

And of course I must acknowledge my oldest child Emma, with whom I was pregnant when I wrote the book. Without that pregnancy I would have never had the time off work to think of writing and illustrating this book. And of course Emma was a very good baby while I finished it.

I must acknowledge my husband Patrick Brown for putting up with me playing around with this idea for so long, and always encouraging me to finish it.

And last and not least I must turn to all our immediate family, children, stepchildren, spouses, partners and grandchildren, because without them around me I would have no reason to do this at all. It is for them.

In age order, we have Emma and her husband Trevor, Joe and his wife Tracey, Sarah and her husband Wally, Max and his girlfriend Andrea, Mark and his wife Yasaman, and Stephanie and her boyfriend Chris Maclelland. And no less important are my six grandchildren—Sophie, Owen, Millie, Oscar, Camila and Diana.

And I also thank those grandchildren that have yet to pop into the world. If I knew your names you would be here too.

INTRODUCTION

By the author and artist
Virginia May

I wrote this book forty years ago. I was still living in London, England. When I started to write it I was married to a young English doctor and pregnant with my first child, Emma. I wrote it to preserve one of the best experiences of my life before my life as a mother started.

The book chronicles my memories of a working summer high up in the Swiss Alps when I was not quite age nineteen. I had found a job working in the Schwarzsee Hotel at an elevation of 8,000 feet. It was my first real travel experience. It took place in 1962.

The hotel is a mountain hotel built as close to the awe-inspiring Matterhorn as anyone other than a rock climber is likely to get. The Hotel is still there, solitary above the tree line.

The Hotel is reached by cable car from Zermatt, unless, of course you want to hike up with your luggage.

The freedom, isolation and beauty that I experienced that sixties summer has stayed with me forever.

I started University in the Fall of 1962 and went back to work again at Schwarzsee during my student years, spent ski holidays there and visited on my honeymoon. Nothing, however, that I have done since has ever quite replaced that fresh learning that comes from first realizing that new worlds and new places are out there for you, waiting to be discovered.

As I write this Introduction in 2014, fifty years later, that ability to be surprised is almost impossible to achieve.

We can all learn about everything instantly, travel cheap, and Skype around the world as the whim takes us. Google is at our fingertips. When the cable car broke down in Zermatt, solitude at Schwarzsee really happened. We could not get on the cell phone, or hook up our laptops to the Internet. None of that was even contemplated. We mailed letters, we didn't text or email, and if we really wanted something fast then we sent a telegram.

I am now a senior citizen, a retired lawyer, living in Western Canada with my Canadian husband. I am a mother of three adult children, three stepchildren, and a growing brood of grandchildren. The Rocky Mountains of North America rise on my doorstep.

I want, in this book, to take you back to fifty years ago when I had the chance to be absorbed into a small mountain community in Switzerland.

I wanted to publish this book in the seventies, when I wrote it, and was close to doing so. The famous English lover of Switzerland, Zermatt, and package holidays, Sir Arnold Lunn had read the manuscript and said that he would write a Forward for the book. The publishers were ready to publish, but then Sir Arnold died.

My life went in another direction. My Canadian life and family took over, as did my law career. I had none of the hours of peace I needed to paint or think about completing this little book project I had started so long ago.

A few years back I retired from law suddenly after having a heart attack and my loving husband of today, encouraged me to start painting again, and I did.

At the same time, I found my old photos, drawings and manuscript, so here you are.

Please enjoy this nostalgic journey with me and breathe in that clear Swiss Alpine air.

MATTERHORN MOUNTAIN SUMMER MEMOIR

1

The Lombardy Express crawled slowly into Brig Station and ground to a halt. It was just before 6 am, and all of my companions in the compartment were sound asleep. I leapt up, dragged my outsize suitcase across their prostrate forms, and landed on the platform just before the train disappeared into the Simplon Tunnel on its way to Italy. The train was gone in a matter of minutes; I was the only person who had got out at this small Swiss border town. The platform was deserted. After travelling for a matter of eight hours or so in a Trans-European train all squashed in discomfort with self-imposed companions, there was something very frightening in watching my temporary home disappear suddenly in a grinding of wheels, leaving nothing but silence in its wake.

I looked around but, unsurprisingly, there was no porter in evidence to carry my suitcase, so I picked it up and plunged down the subway to look for the buffet. Needless to say, it was still closed and so was the bookstall. One place I did not think would be closed was the lavatories and, sure enough, the door opened at a touch. I was feeling so dirty after the all-night trip from Paris that I fell over myself to get into one of the cubicles with sinks and inviting hot water, but the moment I had shut the door I realised that I should have put some money in the slot outside, for it locked firmly behind me. I should have known better. I was locked in and I had only been at large in Switzerland for six minutes. All of my worldly possessions, including my handbag, were on the other side of the door, and nothing I did would make it open. Fortunately, the lavatory was not enclosed right up to the ceiling, so there was nothing for it but to climb over by jumping from the pan onto the toilet-roll holder and so over the top. I was relieved that the lavatory was not one of these hole-in-the-ground affairs that one so often finds in France and Italy, where my jumping-off perch would have been sadly lacking.

I dropped loudly and dustily to the floor on the other side and quickly exited to sit on a cold seat and take stock of the situation in a more leisurely fashion.

The sky was slowly beginning to lighten and the wooded mountains that rose up on all sides around the town looked less menacing in the early morning sunlight. They were only the foothills of the Alps, the beacons announcing the way to the great giants that lay hidden at the top of the lateral valleys that rise up out of the main Rhone valley, but sitting in Brig at that early hour of the day, there seemed nothing paltry about their grandeur. Their sheer mass and height from the valley floor made them as impressive to me as any high-altitude peak that I was to see later.

It was up one of these side valleys that I was about to travel, the Vispertal—the valley that leads to Zermatt and the Matterhorn. I had decided that I wanted to work in Switzerland for a few months before going up to university and had written to the Schweitzer Hotelier Verein in Zurich. After filling out lengthy application forms and what seemed an eternity of waiting, I received a letter from the Schwarzsee Hotel, Zermatt. A brochure was enclosed with the letter but nowhere was there a photograph of the hotel itself, only of swinging cable cars and mountains. From this I surmised that the hotel must be ugly and suspended somewhere on a mountain slope. Sitting back in England, with my knowledge of Switzerland limited to a ten-day visit with the school at the age of fifteen, I had very little concept of where I was going or what to expect. I was not worried. At the age of nineteen or so, everything gets clocked up to experience and there is no such thing as a bad experience, so I was prepared for anything. It was my season for "firsts." I had accepted the job of *Buffethilfe*, or buffet help, without a second thought and set off in mid-June with an enormous suitcase packed with summer clothes, and no trousers or sweaters. This was my wardrobe for a hotel that was situated 8,000 feet above sea level, but I think the fates must have

decided to be kind to me because that summer turned out to be the hottest in about ten years.

I had never worked in a hotel before, either in England or abroad, but I hoped that my experience as a waitress on a few holiday jobs would act in default of actual knowledge. On the other hand, one of the main parts of the application form had asked for knowledge of languages and here I was on more dangerous ground. I spoke school French and was not too worried on that score, but I had also stated on the form that I spoke German. Sitting on Brig Station, I trembled at my presumption, for what I had thought of originally as just an element of exaggeration had now become one enormous lie that was in full danger of being discovered. The Valais canton in which both Brig and Zermatt lie is a bilingual canton, French being the main tongue of the Rhone Valley itself, and German that of the mountain valleys. Zermatt came in the latter category and I was in imminent danger of being found out. I had genuinely intended to teach myself German in the months before my departure. I had solidly worked through the exercises in the *Teach Yourself German* manual, but I had never attempted to vocalize in the language. I need not have worried. The extraordinary vicissitudes of Schweitzerdeutsche defeat even the German nationals, so my ignorance lay masked beneath what sounded like a different language.

It is impossible to enter Switzerland to work without having a medical examination at whichever border town you happen to arrive. I was therefore unable to leave the station at Brig until the medical offices opened at 8 am. So I sat on my cold seat and forcib*ly* meditated. I had all my work permits, but I had been warned that this medical examination was an absolute necessity. Wait in Brig I must, before catching the local train up to Zermatt. How organized the Swiss are! We often grumble about the amount of red tape in England but Switzerland comes a good second.

By far the largest recruitment of foreign workers into Switzerland comes from Italy. Wherever you go, Italians are working on the lower-scale jobs as labourers or as porters and cleaners in the hotels. The Swiss look down on them, but the flow of Italian labour never ceases, particularly through Brig, one of the main reception centres for this traffic since it is situated on the railway line to Milan.

It was getting on for eight thirty and I noticed that the station platform was becoming crowded. Large tattered suitcases lay scattered around, seemingly dropped on the station from the through-train to Paris. The latest batch of immigrant Italian workers had arrived and they, like me, were waiting for the medical examination. I could not understand a word they were saying and I found sitting on the station decidedly embarrassing. There was a continual procession of slowly ambling Italian males passing to and fro in front of me staring in unashamed curiosity, and I found it quite impossible to avoid catching someone's eye by mistake on almost every circuit. Most girls like to be admired and I am certainly no exception, but I began to understand what was meant by too much of a good thing! Unfortunately, there was nowhere to hide apart from the ladies lavatory and my earlier experience there had finished me for trying to get any help from that direction. The Swiss porters who had materialized appeared only faintly amused by the situation. There was nothing for it but to keep a watchful eye for a presentable type and hope that he would act as my bodyguard.

Suddenly the doors of the medical centre were opened and the platform emptied as though by magic. I jumped up and rushed forward, abandoning my suitcase as I did so. I need not have rushed. It was almost impossible to get through the doors for the sea of gesticulating bodies that swam in front of me. I stood patiently at the back of the queue despite having waited for this moment for two hours. At least now I could stand in peace. No one was interested in me any more.

"Prego Signorina." I swung round to find a decidedly attractive young Italian standing very close behind me. I smiled encouragingly. He was just what I was looking for.

He pointed to my suitcase and talked animatedly. In the middle of the musical-sounding phrases that were slipping from his mouth I heard the word *bagagli* and assumed, correctly that he wanted to help me with my suitcase. What joy for me! That suitcase was fast becoming a nightmare. Moving it anywhere was a Herculean task, and most helpful volunteers, I knew, would soon evaporate after the first muscle pull. But not the Italian male, looking for a quick kill. My only problem was to escape with the suitcase before the kill was imminent, and here a different sort of strength was called for: complete resistance in the face of continual persistence.

For the moment, however, I had found a bodyguard, Piedro, also a student, and with some help from him I soon reached the front of the queue and was siphoned off into the female section by a cool Swiss doctor, my passport having been already taken away.

I was the only non-Italian in the changing cubicles and I stood, embarrassingly towering above five or six short Italian wives who were giggling hysterically as they stripped off their black skirts to reveal the most unrevealing of underwear. When I started to strip with them their curiosity rivalled that of their male counterparts, although there was nothing very exciting about my Marks and Spencer slip. Nevertheless, they seemed quite fascinated and stood in an admiring circle, laughing and nudging me to join in the joke, which of course I did, their laughter being so infectious.

It did not take too long to complete the chest x-ray and blood test. I wandered out into the brilliant sunshine to wait for the results and for my passport to be returned. It did not look as though I would be able to get the local train up to Zermatt until at least twelve noon. The heat was becoming intense and my longing to reach that village equally so. Directly opposite the main station of Brig lies the local railway station from which the cogwheel railway departs for Zermatt. I stood looking at the little red carriages with their wooden seats and shrill whistles as they came and went throughout the morning. I hated the delay in getting on that train.

There was nothing to do except explore the town of Brig. I have returned to Brig many times since that morning but the pleasant feeling of that little town has always remained with me. It has grown because of its position, a crossing point on the Rhone for both road and rail connections across Europe to France and Austria, Germany and Italy. It is well stocked with hotels and restaurants and the main street is lined with elegant shops selling more than just the tourist bric-a-brac that is found in other, more touristy Swiss towns. The true glory of Brig, however, is the Stockalper Castle, a magnificent seventeenth-century building lying right in the heart of the town and visible for miles by its three onion-domed towers. Somehow it always seemed to me that there should be a fourth. It was quite by chance that I stumbled into the courtyard of this magnificent building as I meandered around the town.

I was feeling very hot and ahead of me I saw a shaded archway. I stepped beneath it and out into the glaring sun of an open courtyard surrounded on all sides by arcades and balconies filled with geraniums. There was total silence and I stood admiringly, silent too.

It was at that moment that Piedro returned.

"Hallo."

"Hi." That was the extent of our verbal communication, but it didn't seem to deter Piedro. Back at the medical centre he had been momentarily useful and as far as he was concerned I was going to pay for that help with my company. I said a quick farewell to the dazzling, peaceful courtyard and aimed for the nearest café. There is always safety in numbers!

"I think that we had better go back and collect our passports," I said, staring at him full in the face, but Piedro only gazed at me uncomprehendingly, hoping that the liquid expression of his eyes would do something to turn me in his favour.

"Passports," I repeated loudly, and a couple at a neighbouring table in the café looked astonished at the abrupt tone of my voice.

"Ah passaports, si, ma non adesso." I had got through, but the effort was becoming too much and I got up, thanking him for my drink and setting off back towards the station and away from the tempting fields at the back of the town where he indicated that we might walk. He followed behind me like a sulky schoolboy and rejoined his mocking friends on the station steps. That was my first and last attempt to use an Italian male as a bodyguard. Even the most charming and quiet among them seem to desire every female. The trouble is that it really is every female that they desire and this lack of discrimination takes away the first rush of pleasure that any English girl has at being admired in such an obvious manner.

I entered the cool hall of the medical centre and found about forty others all waiting. I sat with the women and waited. It was not long before the polite Swiss doctor returned and began to hand out the passports.

"Carlo Frascati."

"Si signor."

"Romano Bernardi, Vittorio Cadoni, Giuseppe Morelli, Sandro Terranovo…".

The musical-sounding names floated upwards into the high ceiling and the owners of the names sprang forward like genies to grasp their precious green documents once more. The numbers slowly thinned, and then I suddenly heard my own name and saw a royal blue passport on top of the pile. The crowd standing round the Doctor seemed to clear at the unfamiliar name. He smiled pleasantly as I approached and shook my hand.

"I hope that you will enjoy your stay in Switzerland, mademoiselle." His English was perfect and for the first time since leaving home an aura of safety surrounded me.

I was ready at last. I looked at my watch; it was nearly noon. There was just time to catch the 12:10 train to Zermatt, the slow train that stopped at every tiny village on the way up the valley. I staggered with my suitcase across to the waiting Zermatt train. I noticed with relief that none of my fellow immigrants were coming with me. They were mainly going on to work in the larger towns.

I clambered up the high steps into the carriage, pushing the case before me, and sat down on a hard wooden seat. The compartment smelled clean and scrubbed and full of mountain air. It was cosy, small, personal, and soon very full.

There was great activity on the small platform and I noticed that I was very atypical of the majority of prospective passengers. On a very rough division there were two sorts: large, plump local women, their arms bursting with shopping baskets, and equally large, healthy men armed with rucksacks and climbing boots and awkward ice axes that stuck out at every angle and refused to pack away nicely onto the luggage racks. The women were mainly travelling back to their villages after a morning of shopping in the metropolis. The men were climbers, lovers of the high mountains returning for a few days to savour the dangerous joys of the great peaks. I felt like a fish out of water, sitting in my sandals and cotton dress.

There was an air of excitement and warmth. Everyone seemed to know everyone else and greetings were continually exchanged as the laden passengers climbed in and collapsed panting and complaining of the heat in the valley. They were unsophisticated people—unassuming and private. Each gave me a small inclusive nod and then retired peacefully into his or her seat. Their language sounded strange and hard after the lyrical Italian that I had heard around me for most of the morning and there were few words that I recognized, although I knew that it must be German.

The Swiss are always perfectly equipped for whatever activity they undertake and these climbers were no exception. Sitting in the compartment that hot lunchtime, I was tempted to laugh at the great limbs of these men bursting from their three-quarter-length trousers, their thick socks and boots, and the weighty rucksacks that made hunchbacks of them all, but I was laughing in ignorance. How many times during that summer I wished that I had possessed even a quarter of their equipment up in the mountains to keep my feet dry from the melting snows and the swift-descending mountain mists.

The first part of the train journey double-backed along the Rhone Valley, to the small town of Visp. The International night train from Paris had not stopped there on the way through to Brig. At Visp the little red carriages swung sharply southward, following the path cut through the mountains by the river Visp itself. The rise in altitude between here and Zermatt is nearly 5,000 feet, hence the need for a cogwheel railway—a Swiss specialty for coping with steep gradients. Sometimes the gradient lowers the speed of the train to as little as 14 miles per hour, and it is almost possible to pick the blossoming Alpine flowers growing so temptingly on the high banks through which the railway track cuts. The Brig-Visp-Zermatt railway, or BVZ as it is usually written, is a single-track railway for most of its length and the passing places are few. Considering the fact that as many as thirteen trains can go in one direction each day, it is amazing that delays do not occur. Yet I do not remember ever travelling on that journey without departing or arriving exactly on time, even in the cold skiing months, when the banks of flowers are replaced by banks of overflowing snow and the ground is frosted as far as the eye can see. But the joy of this journey is not a result of the technical achievement of carving such a route up the valley flanks, nor of the precision timing of the railway personnel, but of the excitement of the slow rise up into the floating world of the great snow-capped mountains. As the train shoots out of a short tunnel, there are tantaliszing glimpses of well-known peaks and of the enchanting, wild landscape that ranges on every side.

The windows of the train were wide, and the smells of the country drifted into the hot compartment. The lower part of the valley was fairly open, with small hamlets clinging in the distance to the deep hillsides. Just as I wondered how the inhabitants ever reached these suspended chalets, my eyes focused on a cable car wire and there was the solution, an impossibly thin line stretching tenuously across the valley, connecting the people of those villages to the outside world. I think travellers imagine Switzerland as a toy land, where idyllic chalets are set neatly along the lanes, but this part of the Valais canton soon dispels any such idea. The small villages that one passed on the way up to Zermatt were almost, without exception, farm communties, and the thin narrow homes of dark brown wood, amassed in small groupings along the Visptal, bore only a slight resemblance to the musical box chalets we take home as souvenirs. The sloping roof and shutters were purely functional, and the fact that the farm animals were often housed on the ground floor of the buildings during the winter months proved that the life of the inhabitants was a hard life indeed.

The timetable showed that the journey from Brig to Zermatt was scheduled to take about an hour and a half. I settled into the seat to relish the fact that a journey was to take so long, for the distance from Visp to Zermatt was only about twenty miles. Apart from wanting to savour every minute of the scenery, I was quite pleased to postpone my arrival at the hotel for as long as possible. There was no knowing what it would turn out to be like. I craned my head out of the window as we neared Stalden, perhaps the most important town on the way up the valley, for it is here that a branch road goes off to Saas Fee, Zermatt's rival resort in this part of the Valais. At Stalden the journey really became spectacular. Up to Stalden, the train had climbed with the landscape, and the feeling of height was missing.

At Stalden begins the great gorge that leads up to Kalpetran and St. Niklaus. A dramatic arched viaduct crosses the river, carrying the road away from the railway line. Beyond Stalden I watched the cars treading their way along the opposite side of the gorge. The train was going very slowly indeed, as though it were running out of oxygen. My head for heights then was not usually bad, but at certain points, the track literally ran along the very edge of the gorge. Nothing seemed to separate our little red carriage from the swirling water below but the occasional tree stump that had survived the onslaught of progress.

Unfortunately, it seemed always to be at these points that the entire occupants on the side of the train furthest away from the edge moved over to my side to lean far out of the window to get the best view. Their excitement and pleasure was catching but my thrill of excitement was slightly tinged with fear. It seemed impossible that the train could bear the weight of so many large, heavily equipped people all leaning in one direction without tilting right over on its side. I shuddered at the thought, and I shuddered even more when I looked across at the cars twisting and turning along the narrow road to St. Niklaus and heard their horns echoing against the sides of the mountain. Cars cannot go right through to Zermatt but must stop at St. Niklaus, so that from thereon all tourists must travel by train.

Zermatt is car-free. I could not visualize how such a place would be. The valley slowly widened, and in the distance I saw a golden church dome glittering in the warm afternoon sun. It was St. Niklaus, and in the foreground of the church I could see hundreds more objects also glittering in the sunlight. They were the mass of cars that were parked higgledy-piggledy on the undulating grassy plots of land by the railway that served as parking places. Everybody in the compartment involuntarily began to collect their bundles around them more tightly, for it was obvious that there would be a large influx of passengers.

The station was crowded, but this time with a number of tourists ejected from their cars—the dress-and-suitcase type like myself, rather than the rugged mountain species to which the journey was rapidly accustoming me.

My companion in the opposite seat smiled at my look of amazement at the crowds that were intending to invade the vacant space that was left in the compartment. She was a plainly dressed, motherly woman who had sat for the most part of the journey composed and relaxed whilst the rest of the passengers leapt from side to side to catch every scenic view that was offered. She was undoubtedly a woman of the valley returning from her monthly shopping spree. She had been watching me for some time, worried, I think, that I was travelling alone. Our new enforced intimacy as the space in the compartment receded gave her an opportunity to speak.

"Are you going to Zermatt on holiday?" Her English was precise and surprisingly correct, like that of so many Swiss.

"No, to work."

"How unusual!" Her face illuminated and this was the reaction that I always received when I said that I was working. To the Swiss there is something noble about honest work, something preferable to tourism, although of course, it is from the latter that a great deal of their financial security is derived.

"But you are English. I do not remember any English girl working in Zermatt before." I was pleased to hear that. I did not like the idea of going to a little colony of English girls.

"Where are you going to work?"

"At the Schwarzsee Hotel."

"But that is not actually in Zermatt, that is very high you know, right at the foot of the Matterhorn."

The manner in which she stressed the word "high" made me feel that I was going to work in the clouds.

As the train wound on up the valley, I looked out of the window and saw a small hotel clinging to the top of the valley walls, but there was nothing. The fields were close to the train as it dipped and curved its way parallel to the river. The rich scent of pine needles hung in the air and wafted into the carriage. My Swiss friend had relaxed back into her seat, for the noise was now so great in the compartment that further conversation was difficult to hear.

The train rattled along at a fairly fast pace and there were no great dips to frighten my stomach, so I leant out of the window. I felt as though I were amongst the fields and the spiky evergreen trees that swept past within arms' reach. There was little cultivation visible and, outside the small hamlets, few signs of habitation. Every now and then a chalet backed tantalizingly onto the track and once, I saw a family of children playing idly amongst the small allotments that surrounded the building. We were swept past before I could really absorb the scene. I certainly expected every little Swiss girl to look like Heidi, and most of them were fair, but there was nothing so neat and prim about them as about the drawings in my children's book. The little girls that I saw skipping and play-ing and waving to the vanishing train were very suntanned, untidy and poor. Of course, for them school had ended and they had nothing to do but help their parents through the summer, cleaning and farming and tending the few animals that their parents could afford.

The foliage had changed at this altitude—the land was rougher and the trees were mainly evergreen. The sides of the valley were real mountains now, rocky and with banks of dirty brown snow occasionally piled along the river's edge. In some parts I saw the obvious remains of an avalanche, as rocks and tree trunks lay strewn and flattened, forming a sudden clearing in the woods. The air was cooler and a few windows were closed in the compartment.

There was a shrill whistle and the train came to a quick halt in a small vil-lage. Perhaps it was Zermatt already. I leant out of the window. No, this was Herbriggen and nobody but the guard climbed out, and he climbed back in again almost before the train had time to stop and start. I had hardly realized that we were in a village at all before we had gone and Randa was around the next bend.

"There is only one more village, Tasch, and then we reach Zermatt itself," my Swiss friend shouted across to me. I was glad that she had forestalled my anticipation. Tasch looked a charming place, small and unspoiled, and I watched the paved road curling its way into the village centre with some envy. A train journey can be very frustrating. You are dragged relentlessly on to a predetermined destination and must leave behind unvisited so many tempting bends in the road. But then I was not really on holiday. I was coming to work.

I could see that work was going to be very difficult in such a setting.

Between Tasch and Zermatt the train set off at a fair pace and rattled along as though it could contain its excitement no longer. Suddenly it plunged into a tunnel and the scenery was blocked away except for a few glimpses as the tunnel opened on one side and became a gallery. The noise was deafening and my fellow passengers were almost uncontrollable. I kept hearing the word "Matterhorn" drop into the air as they leapt across the compartment and hung out of windows, nearly hitting their heads against the concrete pillars of the gallery. I gathered from their antics that at any moment there would be a sudden view of this mountain, the glory of Zermatt and the pride of the Alps.

The Matterhorn is probably the most photographed and recognized mountain in the world, appearing on chocolate bars and in a replica form in Disneyland. The Matterhorn has the natural shape of a child's imaginary mountain drawing, a perfect triangle.

To a real mountain enthusiast, and one does not have to be a climber to be an enthusiast, there is no possibility of reducing the thrill of expectation whilst waiting to see such a great mountain for the first time. It is rather similar to the experience of first seeing a great painting like the Mona Lisa. No matter how many times one sees reproductions, there is no substitute for the real thing, and no diminishing the impact once seen.

I am a real mountain enthusiast. Even when I hear the word "mountain" I can see it always as though written in large capitals, and it evokes for me all of the sounds and smells of an Alpine scene. There was no danger that to me something as glorious as the Matterhorn would be debased by too much advance publicity.

I restrained myself from trying to find it with my fellow passengers, partly because the effort to compete with them was too great, and partly because I had absolutely no idea in which direction or on which side it would appear. Also I had no wish to have my first view all cramped and crowded. Jealously, I wanted to guard that first moment and keep it to myself. The heavy-built man who was almost sitting on my lap in his efforts to get his neck as far out of the window as possible gave a sudden whoop of joy and then sank back into his seat as though in a state of ecstasy. He was the only person who was successful in catching that first glimpse. In the next moment the train rattled into another gallery and the calm after the storm descended upon us all.

I blinked in the sunlight as the gallery ended. The train was running along fairly slowly now beside a small dirt track, and buildings and chalets were becoming more frequent. I peered out of the window, almost frightened at what I might see. A mountain wall rose in the distance. I had arrived at the head of the valley—the outskirts of Zermatt. The journey was a dead-end journey. There was no way out but back the way I had just come. Across that mountain barrier at the head of the valley lay Italy, but for the moment I had come far enough.

The train became slower and was flanked by utilitarian sheds. It stopped at last alongside another train that was just about to start the journey down. The passengers of the other train hung out of the windows and stared miserably at us. Within a moment they were gone and in their place was a steep mountainside.

The time had come to climb out, but I hesitated to be the first because I did not know what I might find. I held back, smiling a quick farewell to my Swiss companion, who seemed uncertain whether to stay or leave me. Finally she went and I tumbled out of the train with my suitcase behind a mass of heaving rucksacks. For the second time that day I felt very alone, as I abandoned the warmth and security of the small train.

From where I stood I could see nothing of Zermatt, because I was at the very end of the platform. The air was sharp and took my breath for the moment—I had yet to acclimatize to the altitude.

I thought at first that the station must have been on fire, for I could think of nothing else to account for such noise, chaos and gathering of people as confronted me on the platform of this small Alpine resort. In fact, it was the usual sort of scene that greeted every train arrival and departure during the season, as I was to discover later. Everybody was being met by someone, and there was still a crowd of people hanging about after waving goodbye to those departing on the Brig-bound train.

I had to reach the Schwarzsee Hotel by means of a cable car journey, but where the cable car station was situated I had yet to discover. The German Secretary of the hotel had written to me suggesting that I should take a taxi from Zermatt station, but since there were no cars in Zermatt I had been rather bemused by this suggestion.

Feeling just as bemused now, I trundled along in the wake of the crowd towards the spot where everyone was going. Suddenly the station buildings ended and the platform became a large square opening straight onto the main street. I was entranced by the view that greeted me. There in front of me was drawn up a magnificent array of horse-drawn carriages complete with uniformed drivers. The horses were stamping and pawing at the ground as the luggage was loaded on. Each belonged to some hotel and before I could fully adapt myself to the spectacle, I was approached by a number of hotel touts who appeared eager to remove me and my suitcase in the direction of their own carriages. I searched in vain for anything belonging to the Schwarzsee and then noticed at the end of the line a few marked "Taxi." So that was the sort of taxi I had to take, the horse-drawn variety.

I hovered painfully behind the last stragglers from the train, unwilling to make any positive move. The sight before me was too overwhelming, and everybody except me seemed to know what to do.

I do not know how long I stood there just watching, but when I next looked up there was only one vehicle still left in the square. I moved hastily forward but then noticed that there were passengers already in it. The small group turned towards me and the taxi driver called out.

"Where do you want to go?"

"To the Schwarzsee cable car station."

A short conference took place and then, "Come, I can take you," and the occupants started to shift over to make room for me. I clambered up rather precariously and sat down next to a young woman holding a newborn baby. Opposite was the proud father. They were Zermattens returning from the maternity hospital in Visp with their new offspring and I was privileged to ride with them as they returned. I saw little of the village for the hood of the carriage was up to protect the baby and young mother, but the procession was very slow, for at every few yards there was a momentary pause as greetings and congratulations were exchanged with passing acquaintances and shopkeepers. The courtesy that they had extended to me made me no longer feel a stranger in Zermatt.

2

❦

The village of Zermatt seemed very silent after the noise of the railway station, as though the entire population had migrated with the last train down. The only sounds were those of the horse's clattering hooves and harness bells. It was mid-afternoon and the village was sleeping off the effects of a large Swiss lunch.

I sat cramped with my companions, peering out under the hood of the carriage. The street was long and straight and flanked by shops and hotels, but I was limited in my viewing to occasional glimpses of coloured awnings and shop windows. On that first shared taxi ride, Zermatt still remained a place in my imagination. I had not yet seen the Matterhorn, for at the station my eyes had remained firmly fixed at street level. I exchanged only smiles with the young Swiss couple, for it seemed an intrusion on my part to be travelling with them at all and I preferred to stay on the periphery of their journey.

The actual distance we had travelled was short, and when the carriage came to a halt in a small square the young couple departed. The taxi driver turned the horse sharply round and we set off, this time at a fast trot. I looked out beneath the carriage hood and saw the swirling waters of the Visp below, and way above, for the first time, I saw the Matterhorn floating gracefully over me.

It was so like the photographs that I had seen that I could not believe that it was really there; so like the photographs, and yet so much more magnificent, so large and dominating. It was June and the Matterhorn was covered in snow, a complete white queen overpowering the village. Everything else was unimportant.

I had never realized what a powerful force a mountain is up close and how much Zermatt literally lay at the Matterhorn's foot and in its shadow. Despite the presence of many other four-thousand-metre peaks in the area, no other snow peak is visible from the village and this increases the magic of the Matterhorn.

Its splendid isolation demands complete worship and from that second, I became a worshipper. I could not understand how my taxi driver could rattle on across the bridge at such a pace and not even glance at the magnificent view.

The Schwarzsee cable car station lies some distance on the northern bounds of Zermatt and I had a chance to see the Matterhorn many more times on the

17

way there. The road to the cable car station followed the line of the river up towards the mountains and there, between the tall pines along the riverbank, I saw the mountain rising proudly and ostentatiously. The brochure description of the Schwarzsee Hotel had said *"am fusse den Matterhorn,"* at the foot of the Matterhorn. How anything could be nearer than I was at that moment I could not imagine, but then that is one of the great tricks of mountains. In reality you are never quite as near to them as you feel. They lower themselves to your level only to retreat a few more hundred feet for every puffing footstep towards them. It is the only way that mountains manage to retain their mystery despite the hordes that climb up their stony surfaces every summer.

"Well, Fraulein, this is the Schwarzsee cable car station," said the taxi driver as he jumped down and came round to me, pointing towards a grey building at the end of the road. "What are you going to do up there?" he asked, nodding in the direction of the Matterhorn.

"I am going to work in the hotel for the summer."

"It is very quiet up there you know; nothing to do in the evenings." He spoke confidingly. "You want to be down here in Zermatt, plenty of dancing down here."

"But I don't mind being quiet if there are mountains around me."

He looked at me disbelievingly. "The last cable car descends at about 6 pm and that's it, no transport after that."

His finality made it sound frightening, but I was quite determined not to agree with him before I had seen for myself. He helped me down and we stood chatting for a while. The speed at which we had driven on the last part of the journey now seemed totally unnecessary, as it was plain that he was in no rush to get back to the station. I asked him if the hotel was visible from where we were standing.

"Yes, you can see it up there on the horizon." I followed the direction in which he was pointing and saw, way above me across the fields and intervening woodlands, a tiny dot on the ridge. That was the hotel. I could see nothing except its position from where I stood, but what a position that was. It was another three thousand feet above Zermatt at eight thousand feet—right, as the brochure had said, at the foot of the Matterhorn.

It must be one of the highest situated hotels in Europe. From the village it was impossible to look up at the Matterhorn without seeing this small insignificant dot just to the left, perched as though it were about to fall down the mountainside into the village below. The treeline stopped far below the hotel and there were only traces of small mountain tracks running on above the forests, with the occasional glint of metal as the sun reflected on the cable car wires that hung suspended between the summit station and the village where I stood.

"It certainly does look rather lonely up there," I mumbled half to myself, trying to hide a shiver.

"Never mind," said the taxi driver, endeavouring to cheer me up. "Here is my card. If ever you come down to Zermatt one evening when you are off duty, ring me at this number and I will take you out dancing." Dancing was obviously his passion, but it was comforting to hold the card in my hand and feel that I had some contact with the outside world. Looking up at Schwarzsee, I began to feel that in leaving Zermatt, I was leaving a metropolis of enormous proportions.

I felt no more confident when I stood inside the station waiting for the cable car to swing me up to my place of work.

I had never been in a cable car before and it looked a very nerve-racking affair altogether. The cable cars swung out and upwards towards the sky on such incredibly narrow wires that I felt breathless even watching. When one eventually came down and settled beside me on the landing platform, however, it seemed much larger and more solidly built than it had floating in the air. It could hold about fifty inside, but I was glad not to be experimenting with capacity tests that afternoon. A nice empty corner in which I could safely hunch my belongings and myself was all I wanted. I was the only passenger.

Until one understands the Swiss, they can be rather disconcerting in their cool and contained manner. Their sense of humour can be even more difficult to understand, or even recognise as such. As an only child, I was always very bad at recognizing teasing at any time, and now I became the target of the gentle jokes of the cable car men, the ticket collectors, and the conductors. They were a delightful bunch, who became my firm friends and allies during that long summer, always ready to collect things for me in Zermatt when I was unable to get down to the village and always there to cheer me up with their humour. Waiting on the platform for my first ride up to Schwarzsee they nearly reduced me to a lump of jelly with their jokes and comments, most of which I swallowed whole and undigested.

I was very excited but many comments such as "Surely you are not going to work up in that place, a young girl like you? " were not guaranteed to give me the confidence I wanted. The moment that I was within the little silver cabin gliding upwards on the last lap of my journey, however, the enthralling views that surrounded me on all sides made me forget everything except my surroundings. The only noise was a slow whine of the cable. We hung insulated above the earth, and as I gazed downwards at the small hamlets immediately beneath us, I felt that we had been removed from their world and were onlookers only.

The cable car journey was in two stages, for at Furi the first cable car stops and I had to change to another cable car for the final trip to Schwarzsee. Furi is no more than a collection of chalets lying beneath the woods that cover the mountain slope on the outskirts of Zermatt, but it looked very idyllic as I floated slowly down towards it. A number of the chalets had been converted into small bars and restaurants and their terraces lie open to the sun and the slopes of the Matterhorn. The countryside was pure alpine in the true sense of that word.

As far as I could see, there was nothing but grassy meadows sparsely populated with cattle. The fields were crisscrossed with small paths that undulated upwards and wound their way around the occasional clusters of chalets claiming the titles of hamlets, with two small white painted chapels serving a population of hardly more than twenty. In every direction the mountains stretched away behind, providing the perfect backdrop for a painting. A few walkers were visible toiling slowly along the paths. The rise in altitude between Zermatt and Furi is around a thousand feet, although from my position in the cable car it was difficult to see how hilly the ground was beneath.

At Furi I said farewell to my first friends running the cable line and met those

who were to continue the journey. I climbed into the second silver cabin accompanied by a blonde, round-faced cable car man and swung off on positively the last lap of my journey. This time I felt quite seasoned as we drifted upwards, but the gradient suddenly became much steeper than it had been for the journey as far as Furi. The mountainside rose sharply and the cable car pylons clung to the edge. As I reached each pylon there was an uncomfortable bump and my stomach sank and jumped back. The scenery below was no longer gentle and green. The trees had ended, leaving nothing but grass-covered mountainside. The same paths I had seen below continued, but the ground looked hard and stony and everywhere there were patches of snow and small rivulets formed by the snow that had already melted.

My ears popped and my eyes widened and then suddenly I saw the Monte Rosa appear over to my left with the Gornergletcher running down from its base. The Monte Rosa is in fact the highest mountain in Switzerland, but it is invisible from Zermatt itself, so its fame is not so great as that of the Matterhorn. It looked so beautiful that afternoon and so grand.

The Monte Rosa massif is part of a chain of high mountains that lies around Zermatt along the Italian border. The chain consists of a group of four thousand metre peaks, a very significant height for alpine climbers to scale. Indeed, it is impossible to look at the Monte Rosa without the eye drifting on towards the Lyskamm, Castor and Pollux, and the Breithorn. Of course, the Matterhorn (or Monte Cervino, as the Italians call it) is part of that chain too and belongs as much to Italy as to Switzerland, but a break occurs in the chain before the Matterhorn is reached. The Theodule Pass provides a crossing point between the

mountains into Italy and it is this pass that separates the Matterhorn from its fellow mountains and makes it so unique. The other mountains flow magnificently into one another, but nothing flows into the Matterhorn. I did not know the names of the other mountains as I glided slowly upwards on that first ascent to Schwarzsee. I gasped and exclaimed at each new view and continually sought aid from the cable car man in identifying them. I had never seen so much snow or such a glut of Alpine peaks. I was really amidst the arc of Swiss giants along whose ridges runs the Swiss-Italian border.

I stole the occasional glance back down the valley to Zermatt and saw yet more great snow peaks that had suddenly become visible as I gained height: the Dom, the Weischorn, and the Mischabel. I was loose amongst the Alps and I revelled in every moment.

Immediately ahead of me, the mountain rose suddenly, rocky and bare, and the cable car slowed down. It looked as though we could go no further. We hung face to face with the rock wall, and I looked for a way out. We rose against all the laws of gravity, slowly pulled by the thin cables until the terminal station lay just a few yards ahead with the Schwarzsee Hotel itself visible just behind it. The Matterhorn was now much closer and had changed in shape, no longer rising magically above me but now growing out of the ground around my feet. The cable car almost stopped, and then very slowly edged its way into the landing bay, gingerly docking with a slight bump that sent some horned mountain sheep stumbling away from the stones against which they had been grazing. They were the only sign of life.

I was impressed by the hotel as I exited from the cable car station. It was a low, three-storey building with first-floor balconies and a long sun terrace with brightly painted chairs all polarized towards the Matterhorn. It had a chalet-style roof and the whole was white and gleaming. It was inviting and incongruous in this setting, so utterly modern and respectable, surrounded by nothing but stony footpaths and wandering mountain sheep. Snow was everywhere, much purer and fresher than the snow that remained lower down, and I had to step carefully in order to avoid slipping. The cable car conductor escorted me along the short route from the station, carrying my dreadful suitcase in a brave attempt to make it seem no heavier than a handbag.

There were no other buildings in sight. The hotel was on a small flat plateau framed by mountains on three sides; and the fourth side lay the way back down to Zermatt. If I had been looking for the most isolated spot in the world to work, I could not have made a better choice. Only the Swiss could have built such a modern hotel in such a position. There was a sharp bite to the wind and the air around me stung as though it had just escaped from a refrigerator. I felt very stupid with just a cardigan for protection, and my feet looked even more ridiculous as I stubbed my bare toes on the loose pebbles that scattered the paths.

There was wildness about the landscape that made the small hamlets lower down seem very far away, and the brilliant sunshine that was throwing the mountains into such magnificent relief did nothing to soften the picture. The clarity of their outlines only highlighted their rugged personalities. The dips and falls of the small plateau extended to the first rocky outcrop of the Matterhorn base and I could just see a small path winding and reappearing amongst the boulders on its way upward. The Schwarzsee Hotel lies directly on the Swiss climbing route for the Matterhorn summit via the Hörnli Ridge, as well as the route by which it was first conquered, by the Englishman Edward Whymper and his party, in 1865. I do not intend to go into great detail on the story of that climb and the misfortunes that befell its heroes, but it was an exciting thought to know that Schwarzsee Plateau was a staging post on that journey.

My feet resounded heavily as I stepped onto the rough wooden base of the sun terrace that lay in front of the hotel. I picked my way past the chairs and tables that were empty of customers, for it was too early yet for the summer season to have got underway. With a few more steps, I had reached the main door and stepped across the threshold into the hotel. The moment was almost as exciting as when, a few years later, I entered my own house for the first time— the same feeling of proud possession was there. The conductor from the cable car closed the door behind me and let out a sigh of relief as he lowered my suitcase to the ground.

I stood inhaling a new smell of scrubbed floors and polished wood. Everything around me shone with cleanliness and smelt as though it had been plucked straight from the forests that I had passed on the way here from Zermatt. I felt engulfed by the insulated warmth of the hotel and immediately forgot how chilled I had been a moment before.

I was standing, not in a foyer or hallway, but right in the middle of a large, open-plan self-service restaurant, filled with wooden tables and chairs and with red clustered lamps hanging from wooden brackets on walls and ceiling. Beyond, I could see a smart restaurant, slightly partitioned off and laid as though for dinner. Straight ahead of me was the self-service buffet itself, long and low and made of shining steel. A postcard rack hung by the entrance to the buffet bar, and bottles of herbal liqueurs were lined up temptingly in the glass-fronted cupboards behind. A delicious smell of continental coffee mingled with that of the wood furniture. I had never stepped into a hotel like it before. My visits to English hotels had led me to expect the usual type of foyer manned by a small impersonal reception desk, and carpets fitted wall-to-wall that disappeared once you rounded the corner out of sight of the main entrance. There was no porter in sight, or wandering helper. In fact, there was no one visible at all. Neither guest nor staff seemed to exist, for it was the hour of the afternoon rest.

It was a mountain hotel and the etiquette of ordinary hotel life was missing. It was a shelter and lookout point and a place to eat and a place from which to rise at 5 am to see the sunrise. The fact that one could do all this at 8,481 feet with the utmost comfort and pleasure is a credit to the Seiler family of Zermatt, who in the sixties owned the Schwarzsee, along with several other larger and more glamorous hotels in the village. The Seilers were and remain professional hoteliers. It was a member of their family who opened the first hotel in Zermatt, the Monte Rosa.

It is to this tradition that the Schwarzsee Hotel belongs, and Bernard Seiler the present generation of that family found it no effort to visit the hotel on several occasions whilst I was there, to check on its success, despite his other business commitments. It was good to feel that the hotel was a Zermatten's concern and not just a moneymaking enterprise of some outside entrepreneur.

I stood alone in the middle of the restaurant after the cable car conductor had rushed back to take down the next scheduled trip, when Frau Huber appeared, rushing like a whirlwind through the swinging doors that led to the upper parts of the hotel. She flew across the floor towards me panting and smiling, and enveloped me suddenly in her motherly grasp. She was the manager of the hotel, a plump Swiss woman who looked to be in her late fifties or even older. I breathed a sigh of enormous relief when I met her. After all the jokes and teasing on the way up to Schwarzsee,

Frau Huber was charming. She was utterly disarming in her immense pleasure at meeting me and totally surprising in her appearance. With her short gingery hair wisping round her face, and her fringe meeting her glasses she reminded me of a very plump Pekinese. Her features were small and her nose snub and this rather childish face was sitting on top of a large body that appeared more shapeless than it was because of the floral cotton coverall that she was wearing. Her shoes were thick and heavy and her skirt was long. I felt so safe and was so amazed to find such a person running the hotel. Frau Huber came from Zurich, which I discovered later, but she was a mountain lover and had spent most of her working life in small mountain hotels, where she could create the sort of family atmosphere that she did not have at home—she was a widow with no children. In between seasons she would return to her flat in Zurich, where she lived alone. Her greatest pleasure there was to receive letters from staff that she had employed and to hear of their marriages and futures.

She was completely without guile, and yet her insight into her workers was very shrewd. As a woman in charge she had to be doubly strong, and although she was always very kind with me, she was not by any means soft. She was very excitable and her unending energy often seemed to confuse more than to help when the hotel was crowded. I sometimes wish that I had known her when she was a little younger, but when I first met her she was nearing the last few years of her active working life and I think that she sometimes found the hectic amount of work and the problem of keeping both staff and guests at an equilibrium rather a strain. I was very fond of Frau Huber, and rather enjoyed her quick flashes of temper, even when directed against myself, because she was so genuinely good-natured that her tempers were soon past—I had only to talk of her beloved Swiss mountains or praise some particularly delicious Swiss fruit flan that she had personally made and all thoughts of anger would disappear. Her English was very pidgeon and spiced with Swiss phrases. She was obviously looking forward to improving it with me over the summer. She clasped my hand tightly in welcome and revolved me towards the light, so that she could see me properly.

"Well, I am pleased that you have arrived safely. I hope you will enjoy yourself here, but you have to work hard you know. It is very busy when the season has started. Sit down; I'm sure you must be very hungry. What would you like to eat? Have you had any lunch? Would you like a piece of flan and a coffee? You must be very tired and you will find it very difficult to get used to the altitude. It will make you very sleepy for the first few days. You are not used to mountains in England, eh? You are the first English girl to come and work at Schwarzsee. We have a lot of English guests in Zermatt. Have you ever been here before eh…" Her conversation ran on and on and all the while she bustled and fussed around me, pushing me into one of the tables in front of the buffet and cutting a piece of flan and then pouring coffee, spilling it into the saucer in her haste to hand it over the counter. She was not silent for a moment, and I just opened and shut my mouth and in the end decided to shut it permanently, for it was plain that I was not expected to answer anything at all.

"Now you must go straight to rest for you will be starting work tomorrow morning and you will need your sleep, eh. We start very early here you know, five am, so you must get a lot of sleep. You will be on your own for a few days but then you will be sharing your bedroom with an Italian waitress that we have coming. Of course at the moment you will be in a guest room for we have no guests, but never mind. Oh how I wish Fraulein Stringer were here. Her English is very good you know. She worked in England for a year. She comes from Hamburg. She is a little older than you are, but I am sure you will like her. She is looking forward to meeting you."

The names and facts came tumbling out and I sat and listened, only taking in a quarter of all that she was saying. I remembered the name Stringer as that of the German secretary who had sent me the work contract and was glad to hear that she was young. I felt I should need a companion. The thought of sharing with an Italian was not quite so enthralling, as my experiences down at Brig had shown me that not many Italians speak English. I wondered in what language we would communicate, for I spoke no Italian at all. The fact that shone out to me loudest and clearest was the phrase, "work at five am." I thought at first that Frau Huber had made a mistake in her English, but that did not seem very likely, since the word for five in English differs little from the German. The only people I had ever known who started work at five were milkmen. I paled at the thought and almost fell asleep at the prospect. Of course, there was no danger that I really would fall asleep through the flow of information. Frau Huber was quite determined that I should not lack for knowledge.

"We shall be quite an international group here at Schwarzsee this summer, eh. There is a Yugoslavian girl here, and a Spaniard and two Austrian girls are coming in a week's time, and we have several Italians to do the heavy work so you can see we are quite an international little family. Now I must stop talking and let you go to sleep. Leave your suitcase here and the boy will bring it up later. I will show you to your room."

She stopped talking with an abruptness that left me breathless and suddenly charged off towards the swinging doors. I followed behind, dragging my suitcase with me, for I was quite determined not to be parted from it now, despite her instructions. Beyond the swing doors I found myself in a small hallway leading one way to the staircase and the other to the side door for guests coming directly to the hotel rather than to the restaurant. It was an entrance that looked as if it was not used very much. We climbed to the first floor and then on again to the second. Everything looked new and so clean that I began to worry at the amount of work needed to keep it so clean. I hoped that it was not going to be one of my jobs. Although my contract had said that I was employed to work on the self-service buffet, it was clear that in a hotel of this size, everyone would have to help out and that if anyone were to have a day off, then someone else would have a double work load for that day. I was getting the feel of things pretty quickly.

"There, here is your room. Now I must go back to mine, and have a rest. We shall be eating at about 7 pm and then you can meet the rest of the staff." Frau Huber flung open the door of the room ahead, smiled, and vanished further along the corridor. There was not a sound in the hotel and I began to wonder if she and I were the only occupants.

I stared through the open doorway at the room, which I was to share with this unknown Italian. It was small, pretty, and bright. The beds and the entire woodwork were of a pale pine-coloured wood, and small red shaded lamps were on the bedside tables. There was a writing table and two chairs, a built-in wardrobe, and a sink. The beds were covered with thick white eiderdowns.

The whole effect was so spotless that I felt frightened to put my foot over the threshold.

I moved slowly to the window, pulled back the fragile net curtains, and flung open the shutters. There, staring me full in the face, was the Matterhorn, brilliant and as close as though it were a tree in my back garden.

Gorgeous! I collapsed back onto the soft eiderdown, kicking my shoes up to the ceiling and wallowing in the softness and the vicious cold air that swept through the room. I unpacked and within seconds I was lying in my own chaos and the prim room of a few moments before had become my recognizable pad.

3

There was silence everywhere when I woke up from what must have been a short doze—silence and a gripping coldness. I had forgotten to close the window and had made myself a willing target for the biting air.

I jumped up to close it and as I did so I heard a sound from immediately beneath it. My bedroom was on the second floor and looked directly down onto the wide balcony that ran the full width of the hotel on the first floor, and there I could see a pair of female legs stretched out, glistening with sun cream. It must have been a real sun-trap down there, completely protected from the sharp winds by the glass of the open French windows.

I withdrew my head rapidly to avoid being caught prying. I was going to have to start right away remembering that I was not a privileged guest but a worker, someone who should be seen and not heard, until needed. But then I remembered that there were no guests at the moment according to Frau Huber. Those legs must belong to another member of staff. I popped back to the window with increased curiosity and suspended myself out as far as possible to see all that there was to see. I must have made a slight noise for there was a sudden exclamation of annoyance and then a head shot out and stared up, grimacing in the strong sunlight. Quickly a smile broke across the face and a finger was directed at me.

"English Fraulein?"

I nodded.

"Ah." The welcoming grin spread wider, but then, "Sonne...wunderbar," said my fellow worker, pointing in the direction of the sky and then disappearing with a flash of gold teeth back into the recumbent position of a true sun worshipper.

The girl was obviously neither Swiss nor Italian. I wondered where she came from. She looked a very likeable person. She was, I supposed, in her late twenties, with bubbly short brown hair and round pretty features. I wanted to find out at once, but was forced to wait until supper that evening because I did not dare leave my room, in case Frau Huber discovered that I was not asleep as directed.

Long before I gained enough courage to creep down to the supper table, I heard the hotel coming to life and the sounds of banging doors in the distance. I wondered where the staff would eat and what sort of food I could expect. Before leaving for Switzerland I had been told some dreadful tales about the sort of living conditions that workers had to suffer in European hotels, but I was finding it difficult to fit these tales in with my general impressions of the Schwarzsee Hotel, all the more so when I went into the self-service restaurant and saw one of the large wooden tables in the window laid ready for a meal, obviously our supper. Behind the buffet was the girl I had seen on the balcony, now busy slicing a long brown loaf. From the kitchen emanated loud Italian conversation.

Frau Huber appeared bustling from the kitchen, a nylon overall bursting at its buttons across her chest.

"Virginia, you are just in time to eat. You look much better now that you have slept." I did not confess that I had hardly slept at all for the excitement. "You must come and meet Peppita, she is from Slovenia in Yugoslavia." She led me across to the girl behind the buffet and we formally shook hands.

"Virginia is from England, Peppita, she will teach you to speak English." I laughed as Peppita threw up her hands in mock horror and sadly shook her head. She asked if I spoke either Italian or German. To the latter I was obliged to say yes, because Frau Huber was standing right beside me. Peppita was to be my guide on the self-service buffet; I was allocated to her for training. The whole concept of self-service was fairly new to Zermatt then and Frau Huber was very proud of the gimmick. How lucky I was to work with Peppita. She was one of the world's placid kind, born to shrug at disaster. Someone had to counterbalance the excitability of the Italians and the sudden flashes of temper of Frau Huber.

I do not think that Peppita was her proper name but I never called her anything else. She was thirty and unmarried and a permanent itinerant hotel worker—a group of people that I had never really known before, people who travel from hotel to hotel, from season to season, and from country to country, always wanting to learn a language or to make money for some mythical home

of the future, or to find romance and excitement in a continually changing environment. Few of them were married, because marriage does not lend itself well to such a career, and most of them seemed to live with parents between seasons or return to small bachelor apartments as did Frau Huber. Those who worked in the Swiss Alpine resorts were lucky because they had two main seasons a year—the winter ski season and the summer climbing and hiking season. The time between the closing of one season and the beginning of the next was little more than a few weeks. In fact, some hotels in Zermatt stayed open the whole year because of the opportunity for year-round high-altitude skiing.

Friendships were easily made amongst seasonal hotel workers, and as easily broken. Within even a few days, a degree of intimacy could be reached that had little bearing on a permanent relationship, but which at the time was of the greatest importance. The life of the hotel became the only life, and just as on holiday, a definite time limit increased the speed of passions, so that the approaching end of a season acted as the catalyst for fast emotional development.

To these hotel workers, the environment in which they worked was of paramount importance, because the hotel of that season was their temporary home. I suppose this can be said for most live-in jobs, but hotel life is quite unique, for I can think of no other residential type of job where one lives and works with such a cross-section of society. In a hotel, people of all ages are forced to live and eat and work together, from the young kitchen boy to the old hall porter.

At the same time, hotel work by its very nature is global and tends to attract a wide range of nationalities. In England, there are few hotels that could survive the high season without the help of Spaniards and Italians.

Of course, to a great extent the staff of a hotel creates its own hierarchy. With little more than twelve staff members isolated on a mountainside and with no cable car connection to the village after six o'clock, I initially thought that it would be difficult for even the manager to stand on ceremony. Later that evening I learned differently.

In such an environment, the small personal possessions that one takes so much for granted in one's own home really become of prime importance. They are the only things that can turn a shared staff bedroom into something approximating one's own little world. In many ways, I, and the two Austrian girls who arrived later on in my first week, were intruders into this world. If we were not happy, nothing was lost; it was just a question of going straight home and finding something else to fill up the gap before college and bringing in a bit of money. I felt very lucky never to be made to feel an intruder and to be accepted by my colleagues.

The Schwarzsee Hotel was about to have its first summer season when I arrived there. It had only opened the previous winter and had been built on the site of a Victorian hotel of the same name that had been destroyed by fire in 1957. Judging by a few old postcards that I saw in the rack by the buffet, that was no sad loss. Schwarzsee literally means Black Lake, and both the hotel and the plateau on which it stood were named after the small, dark pool of ice-cold water that lay hidden in a hollow a few hundred yards from the cable car station. Frau Huber had come as manager to the hotel right at its beginning and had brought with her Peppita, the German secretary, and the German chef, all from the previous hotel that she had run in Meiringen. The four of them knew each other well and there was a friendship between them that made working so much easier, and I think it was a measure of Frau Huber's success that she managed to bring staff with her in this manner.

It was into this atmosphere that I found myself welcomed that first evening. The secretary, Heidi Stringer, had not yet returned from her climb but was expected to be back before the end of the meal. The chef, Herr Hausmann, was missing when Frau Huber took me into the kitchen before supper to introduce me to the Italians and to the one Spaniard, Antonio, a bald-headed, temperamental washer-up. There were two Sicilian married couples, Valentino and Italia and Guido and Pasqualina, plus Carlo, a young Italian of about my own age. The two couples were employed to do the cleaning and the heavy work together with Carlo, who seemed to be the unofficial porter and general factotum. None of them spoke anything but Italian, and I felt sad to learn that both couples had children living with grandparents whilst the parents came to earn a living to support them. These Italians were another sort of itinerant worker, ones with homes and families who were driven to work abroad through lack of opportunity and a bad economy in their own country. I now understood the looks of anxiety that I had seen on the faces of those Italians with which I had been forced to wait at Brig. Had they been refused entry, the livelihood of an entire family in Italy might have suffered. When I was introduced, the women smiled coyly, but the two husbands appeared more reserved. I hoped that I would get a chance to talk with them properly at supper, but soon found that was not to be.

Frau Huber was busy ladling spaghetti into a big bowl and my heart sank as I imagined trying to master the problems of eating spaghetti when feeling as famished as I was, but the spaghetti was not for me. Valentino took the bowl, and Peppita handed over the bread that she had been slicing, and the entire group of Italians together with Antonio vanished down a flight of stone steps that led from the kitchen to I knew not where. I realized quickly that even with a staff as small as twelve a hierarchy existed at Schwarzsee. Obviously, there were two meal sittings, and I was lucky enough to be in the upstairs one. It may have been that the Italians preferred to eat together as a unit and to stick to eating their traditional Italian food, but when I saw later where they went to eat, in a stone-walled room on a bare table in the basement, I wondered at their ready acceptance of this differentiation. Their bedrooms were right next door to the great, refrigerated storerooms. I had little on which to judge at the time, but later, when I spent a night in a big hotel down in Zermatt, I realized that perhaps my colleagues at Schwarzsee were lucky, for down there in the village, privacy hardly existed at all, people sleeping in virtual dormitories. Obviously, the cushioned existence into which I seemed to have walked at Schwarzsee was not typical.

So Peppita and I were left to sit down alone whilst Frau Huber busied herself in preparing our own supper, as the chef was still missing. Business was obviously slack at the moment. Frau Huber shouted across from the buffet for our assistance and I carried in my first hot meal, a vast tureen of vegetable soup followed by goulash with salad and noodles. It was delicious. Swiss food for me was exactly right, solid and substantial in its helpings, but cooked with a nice continental tinge of spices and sauces.

It was an extraordinary affair, that first meal. There was only Frau Huber, Peppita, and myself sitting down to eat at a table laid for seven. I found it difficult to concentrate on the important task of eating when I was constantly trying to imagine the people who were due to fill the empty places. At the same time, I was continually drawn to the windows on all sides and the spectacular views of the mountains that I could see through them. There was total silence outside, and a magnificence that I had never experienced before. There was a sunset following the lovely day and although it was by no means the most flamboyant sunset that I saw, it was good enough for me that night. We had no lights on in the hotel and sat munching in near darkness, so that the pink haze of the sky and glow of the mountain peaks were visible for as long as possible. The Matterhorn was black and gone long before the Monte Rosa chain, which shone red and glorious after the streetlights in Zermatt were blinking and winking. We were so high up that there seemed to be a whole extra hour of twilight. It was the most solitary setting I had known, and total security lay only within the hotel doors.

A rather dull conversation, judging by the faces of the two protagonists, took place in German between Frau Huber and Peppita, mainly concerned with when the secretary would get back from her climb, and what on earth had happened to the chef. I concentrated on eating.

A sudden laugh and exclamation from Frau Huber made me look up quickly and follow her gaze out the window onto the terrace. There, scarcely visible in the fading light, was a tall, thin middle-aged man in a short white jacket. He was skipping furiously.

"Virginia look, there is Herr Hausmann. He is getting himself ready for supper." Frau Huber giggled girlishly and clutched herself round the waist with mirth.

"That is the chef?" I asked, a little puzzled, looking to Peppita for enlightenment, but she only raised her eyebrows and shrugged as though to exclude herself from the whole affair.

The man was skipping even faster now that he saw us all looking at him, and I began to wonder if he would have any energy left for cooking.

"He is so funny, that man," said Frau Huber, still laughing to herself. She banged on the window and called for him to come and eat. A few seconds passed and then the chef stopped, slowly and deliberately folding up his skipping rope and coming into the hotel.

He advanced towards the table with exaggerated pants, clutching his side as though he were suffering from a stitch. He sank slowly into the chair next to mine and nodded curtly to acknowledge my presence. He seemed to be totally disinterested in me despite Frau Huber's efforts to introduce us. I was not too worried. His morose face and efforts at showmanship did not make me think that he was going to be my greatest friend, and in any case he rather scared me Herr Hausmann was German and I think that I was probably one of the first English people that he had ever had to know for any length of time since the end of the Second World War. He was obviously not yet over the war in his own mind. He was, I suppose, around forty, tall and greying. His sense of humour was strange. He was a bachelor and that, I think, was one reason why he was so odd in his manner towards young girls. I think that his shyness took the form of brusqueness. He had worked before with Peppita and so was at ease with her, but I was something new. In many ways he appeared to have the expected temperament of a chef, but it was difficult to tell whether he really was in a temper sometimes or whether he was just play acting. I found out later that he had two passions in life: physical fitness and Shirley MacLaine. Her pin-ups covered the wall of his bedroom, and that image seemed to be the only woman for whom he could feel any interest. Why he was such a fanatic for keeping fit I never discovered. The stupid thing was, that living as we all were in the mountains, the easiest way to keep fit was to go for a walk, because in whichever direction one set off from Schwarzsee you had to climb either on the outward or return journey. He, however, seemed to prefer muscle-building machines and skipping ropes to the real thing.

At one time I was responsible for tidying his bedroom, because in the hotel hierarchy a chef is, of course, much too high to undertake such a menial task. I was curious, I have to admit, to see what personal belongings he had and whether there were any private photographs or anything that would show why he had not got married, but there was never a thing, nothing but the pin-ups and the health machines.

There were still three empty places at the table and the meal was almost over. The sound of heavy feet on the wooden boards of the terrace made us look towards the window, but the lights were now full-on, casting a soft gentle glow around the dining room, and we could see nothing outside. The door opened and two exhausted creatures appeared, looking exactly like the climbers that I had seen boarding the train earlier that day. From where I was sitting, it was impossible to tell what sex or age they were, for they were wearing so many layers of clothes that all shape had long since disappeared. Frau Huber and Peppita leapt from their seats to help them lower the great rucksacks to the ground and I followed suit, determined not to be left behind. Only the chef remained eating, shouting his comments from the middle distance.

As their anorak hoods dropped down, I was introduced first to Heidi Stringer, the German secretary, and then to her companion, an elderly Swiss mountain guide from the village. I remembered at that moment a Fodor's tourist guide that I had read on Zermatt, in which the author had talked about the handsome bronzed guides who lounged along the village high street waiting for clients, and wondered if the elderly grey-haired man in front of me was more typical of what they were really like. He certainly was bronzed and to my mind far more likeable, for I have always had a weakness for old men, with their rambling tales and slow manner of speech. The old guide looked just that type and far less of an emotional hazard than some suntanned god in his late twenties.

Before long they had joined us with climbing boots off and stockinged feet buried under the table. They were both famished, but Heidi seemed to find eating difficult because her lips had swollen from the reflected glare of snow and sun up on the glaciers that she had crossed that day. Her round cheeks were burnt red and peeling and yet she still managed to look pale and tired. She had returned from climbing the Breithorn, her first four-thousand-metre peak. Her eyes were dancing with the excitement and she could hardly talk fast enough of the day's adventures, but physical exhaustion was quickly taking over. She was about 22 years old, a plain German girl with short, straight mouse-coloured hair and rather heavy features. She seemed very pleased to meet me at last and was full of apologies that she had not been there to greet me. I liked the look of her and was pleased to discover that her English was excellent; she had spent some time working in York and was, I think, very glad to be able to practise it with me.

The conversation definitely took a turn for the better after Heidi's arrival. I was fascinated to see that a girl could climb the mountains with comparative ease and was excited by every word that I heard about the fabulous views from the summit of the Breithorn.

"You can see Mont Blanc from the top," said Heidi, "and of course, on a beautiful day like today, every mountain looked its best. The Matterhorn was quite breathtaking and standing on the summit we looked right down into Italy on the other side of the chain."

I was green with envy as I sat there, thinking that all the time whilst I had been ploughing up the valley with my sandals and my suitcase, gasping at the snow-capped peaks in the distance, these two people eating with me had been standing right on top of one of them. In fact, I had no real conception of the dangers or difficulties that they had encountered. I was, I am afraid to say, at that time a complete novice as regards mountain climbing and my first thought was to rush out and climb the Matterhorn myself. After all, one only needed a guide to show you the way...or so my secret train of thought ran. Something of my wishful thinking must have shown in my face, for the old guide turned towards me then and, patting me on the arm, said, "And you Fraulein, do you want to climb while you are in Zermatt?"

"Oh yes," I replied eagerly, for the first time putting into words my own ambition and admitting it to myself.

"Well, you look strong enough to me. By the time you have been here a couple of months, you may be fit enough to go on your first small climb." I had no idea what "fit" meant, but I nodded wisely.

"Let me know when you feel ready and I will take you myself." He sat back proudly and I thanked him, conscious of the honour that he had done me and aware of Frau Huber nodding encouragingly towards me.

"You are a very lucky girl, you know, Virginia. Herr Taugwalder can charge his clients a great deal of money, and yet he says he will take you for nothing." She was very pleased at the thought of money saving, even if it was someone else's. Nobody ever seemed to mind discussing money matters in Switzerland, and Frau Huber was certainly no exception to the rule.

I was fast discovering over the meal that my role for the first few days was going to be that of silent onlooker in a very new environment. I was having to learn two whole new vocabularies of life, that of the hotel world and that of the climbing fraternity. The first I had been expecting, but of the second I had thought little. Sitting there that evening as I listened to strange words, like "bivouac" and "crampons," "belay" and "crevasse," I became completely caught up on the fringe of the adventure of mountain climbing. I thought nothing of the dangers.

Frau Huber opened a bottle of Fendant to celebrate Heidi's success and the conversation flowed with the wine. Fendant is the local Valaisian white wine grown down in the Rhone valley. I drank a good few cases that summer. Herr Hausmann became loud and backslapping as the wine began to take effect and Peppita flushed and giggled. Even Heidi, whom I judged to be a normally rather reserved person, became exuberant, and of course, Frau Huber and Herr Taugwalder were lost in their own world of dialect and anecdote.

I must have nearly dropped to sleep as I sat knocking back my third glass, and soon I was bundled unceremoniously off to my bedroom with the reminder ringing in my ears that work started at 6 am the following day. Such a thought just made me smile all the more in my new-dazed state. I was very unused to drinking wine at all, let alone in such quantity, and the effect of the long journey and the excitement of the day had taken their toll. I must admit, however, that I never did become hardened to the effect of Swiss wine, and the result of a few glasses was, for me, always the same fantastic gaiety, followed by a splitting headache.

I struggled, stumbling up the wooden stairway with Heidi and Peppita, the three of us holding on to each other for support and trying to carry with us the rest of Heidi's climbing equipment. I was glad to see that her bedroom was almost opposite mine and Peppita was further along the passage. The danger of a night assault by some over-amorous Italian guest or worker would be very limited in its chances of success with such staunch female protection nearby. It was a thought that was ever present in my mind after the adventures at Brig that morning.

As I said goodnight, I suddenly remembered that the seventh place had never been filled at the supper table.

"Who else was there to come?" I asked Heidi.

"Oh, it must have been for Lucas," she replied, "the little Swiss boy."

"How old is he?"

"About eleven."

"But surely he doesn't work at that age."

"Well, he helps to clear the tables and do the washing up. He comes from Visp, but his family is so large that they cannot afford to keep him and feed him during the summer holidays. He is the oldest, you see."

I thought of the children I had seen playing by the side of the railway line on the way up. He must come from such a home.

"But where is he tonight?"

"I expect he has already gone to bed. He shares a room with one of the Italian families and they usually go to bed very early." What a strange arrangement. I wondered at its acceptance by Frau Huber. I was too tired to think anymore, however, and flopped into my bed and snuggled down beneath the huge quilt, as all problematical thoughts floated quickly out of my mind. The last sounds I heard were of Frau Huber steering an inebriated guide to his room for the night because he had missed the last cable car back to the village.

4

It was not until I had started my first week of work at Schwarzsee that I realized why the Swiss are so financially secure and such successes amongst Europeans in managing their own economy. They actually work hard and whilst doing so they make everyone else who comes into the country work equally as hard. Had I been asked to undertake a sixteen-hour working day in an English seaside hotel I am quite sure that I would have called out a union to protect me from exploitation, but sitting up there in the Alps, I never wanted to complain and never even thought of it.

One factor, of course, was that there was little else to do at Schwarzsee except work, particularly in the evenings, unless you wanted to stay in your bedroom, and I much preferred to give a helping hand in the restaurant or behind the buffet, and chat to the guests, conversationally inclined. To me, it was enough to be paid to stay up in the mountains, working or otherwise. How could I grumble at getting up at five every morning to heat the ovens and get the breakfasts ready? By doing so, I was the first to break the silence of the mountains and to watch the sunrise, and to feel the cold, eight-thousand-foot air tingling on my face and hands as I unlocked the hotel, opened the door, and broke the warmth of the night insulated in the hotel. Neither did I ever complain of sometimes being employed as a chambermaid, not mentioned in the original contract, since I never managed to get rid of my excitement at standing on the long hotel balcony, gazing dreamily at distant snow ridges and glaciers, while shaking out the dustpan and sheets to make a room ready for the next guest. Even the guests seemed to breathe the air of the mountains from their pores.

Whether the hotel was very full or the restaurant very busy made little difference to the work timetable for me, for a certain schedule had to be accomplished each day, and with few guests it only meant that the periods of rest in any one day actually did exist, instead of vanishing completely as when the high season got underway. My daily timetable soon followed a recognizable pattern. Breakfast each morning was at seven, by which late hour the rest of the staff had managed to drift into a waking state, with the exception of Frau Huber, who rarely appeared before nine. "Buon giorno," "Guten Morgen," "Buenas dias," the unfamiliar morning greeting soon became a familiar ritual. Nobody

41

ever bothered to say "Good morning;" I was the one that adapted. Breakfast was always the same—two large jugs of coffee and hot milk and a great mound of brown bread served with unsalted butter and cherry jam. The first week I could manage only a couple of slices each morning, but before I returned to England I was packing myself full of at least six slices a sitting, and the remarkable fact was that not an ounce of weight did I put on, due no doubt to the enormous amount of physical activity that my work involved. I just could not resist that jam with the original fruit still recognizable, unlike the usual puree type of jams that I was used to.

The coffee, or rather its preparation, however, was my regular morning headache. It was filtered coffee and was prepared in a fairly complicated machine that took a very long time to heat up; that was one reason that I had to start work so early in the mornings—to enable the machine to be hot enough in time for breakfast. The first day that Peppita showed me how to work it, I thought that I should never master its inlets and outlets. I didn't dare oversleep because the tepid taste of uncooked coffee would have been too much of a giveaway.

I remember one day, when the hotel inspectors and architect were due to visit, being especially primed by Frau Huber to keep the coffee flowing and have enough prepared at all times. I was determined to please and kept up a continual supply of coffee-filled canisters to fix on the top of the machine. Unfortunately, I had forgotten the all-important task of slipping in the thin filter papers between the coffee container and the water container, with the result that grains of cof-

fee trickled slowly down into the narrow capillary tubes and completely clogged up the machine. No coffee came out and none could go in. I disappeared or rather, was pushed forcibly out of sight by a hysterical Frau Huber, who mounted a stool with a mass of tiny wire brushes and tried to repair the damage before the next cable car arrived, bringing with it the feted visitors. It was the sort of painstaking repair job that needed calmness, a placid temperament, and no time limit. The flailing brushes as wielded by Frau Huber that morning were destined to be unsuccessful and I sulked in disgrace whilst the visitors sipped ordinary Nescafe and heard of the familiar trials of employing inexperienced staff. I hated to appear so incompetent, but mistakes were an inevitable part of learning a job and even the best made them.

On one occasion when the self-service buffet was very busy at lunchtime, with a queue stretching almost to the door, Frau Huber came rushing in from the restaurant to look for a bottle of special wine that she had stored in the deposit beneath the counter. She was hot and excited and her cheeks were flushed with the thought of the crowds and the profit that the hotel was making. When she at last unearthed it, she was determined to open the bottle immediately. There was a loud retort and the cork shot into a group sitting at a table nearby, while the wine itself, which had over-fermented, flew upwards in a graceful fountain and scattered on everything far and near—guests, staff, glasses, postcards, cakes, and cheese. Everything in sight within a radius of several yards was bespattered with red wine. The lovely brown wood ceiling of the buffet bar and the shelves that ran along its back were stained with a perma-nent tint of red. The horror of that moment was too much. Many of the guests in the self-service restaurant were collapsing with laughter but I was not. Frau Huber looked as though she too would soon erupt in a simi-lar display to the wine and I wanted to be as far away as possible when that might hap-pen. Only the chef dared stick his head in from the kitchen and make some rather inopportune joke.

I was glad I was not the only one that seemed to cause a little havoc now and then.

One part of the hotel machine where my talents did not shine forth was in the bedrooms. I hated, hate now and always shall hate, housework, and housework as required by Frau Huber's exacting standard was a terrifying undertaking. After morning breakfast I usually went to do the bedrooms. I learned to hate the one-night guests. All that new bed linen nearly reduced me to tears of exasperation and temper.

"Well Virginia, how are you getting on upstairs?"

"Fine, thank you, Frau Huber," I replied on my third morning, getting ready to lay the staff lunch table.

"Have you finished the bedrooms then?" She sounded somewhat disbelieving.

"Oh yes, they are all done."

"Completely?" Her insistence made me begin to doubt whether I had really done the tasks properly.

"I think we shall go on a little tour of inspection together, gel?" She always used this dialect word at the end of her questions and I learnt to dread its persuasive powers. I just knew that she would find some little thing that was wrong, but together we gathered up the room keys and solemnly mounted the stairs in single file to the amusement of Peppita, who winked at me as she lolled in a leisurely manner over the bar.

Only one of the main guest rooms on the first floor had been slept in, by a zealous one-night mountain viewer, and he seemed to me hardly to have touched the bed, let alone slept in it. Frau Huber paused knowledgeably in his vacated room.

"You have not changed the cover on the quilt."

"But it's not dirty."

"It is creased." I tried to see a small tuck in the material but Frau Huber was already fiddling with the strings and ripping the cover off. To the locals those quilts were easy to manage and certainly they were delightfully warm to sleep beneath, but when it came to folding them neatly in half on a single bed and getting them inside a clean cover I was completely defeated. They were at least four times the size of a normal pillow and I always had enough trouble getting a pillow right down into the corners of its case. That was just the beginning. The inspection parade had started.

"You must polish the taps on the bath, get a new bulb for this lamp, replace the tissues in the container, provide more hotel notepaper in the folder on each table, make sure the blankets are neatly folded, get another towel for the wash basin, and dust, Virginia you have not dusted the lampshades..." The voice went on and the list became longer. I tried to let my eyes slide past Frau Huber towards the Matterhorn's shimmering outline, which was her backdrop through the window, but somehow nothing managed to drown out the voice of the perfectionist at work training her new member of staff. The rooms were being prepared for the summer influx after their hibernation and they had to be perfect.

"You know, Virginia, you will have to know how to do all these things properly when you become a housewife, so you can now learn from me." I did learn and I did listen and I suppose I must grudgingly admit that the results were worth the effort. Whenever during the rest of the season a casual visitor to Schwarzsee would ask to see the bedrooms with a view to staying the night instead of returning to Zermatt, I always felt proud at the gasp of admiration that greeted the key turning in the lock as the door was flung wide. There was such an air of civilization about the bedrooms that it was impossible to believe that the hotel was really only classified as a mountain hotel and was without a proper lounge. The comfort and cleanliness of the rooms, and the panoramas that they commanded, made them instantly tempting to the guest.

Of course, the second gasp usually came when I told them the price, for it was not cheap to stay at Schwarzsee. I often found it was better to tell them the price first and then, whilst they were still laughing in derision at such a price being charged in such an isolated spot, they would lose their breath with sudden wonder at the Matterhorn overflowing into the bedroom, the gushing hot water, the sparkling bedside tables, and the feeling of light and warmth combined.

I did not work in the bedrooms for long, however, because two Austrian girls arrived from Klagenfurt and I was relieved of my duties in that direction and allowed to work more on the buffet. I enjoyed working on the buffet because of the contact that it gave me with the guests, the larger tips, and the continual comings and goings throughout the day. The two Austrians, Gherda and Gherlinda, were students like myself, but their arrival did not add to the harmony of the hotel. Because they were travelling together, they never became as integrated with the other staff as I did alone.

I must admit that I never particularly liked either of the Austrian girls, although by age and background they appeared to be my natural companions. They also spoke English. They were complainers and never recovered from the fact that they were asked to undertake housekeeping work, which had not been mentioned on their original contracts. To look at, Gherlinda was the more attractive, a tall slender blonder with very blacked-in eyebrows. Gherda on the other hand was short, busty, and olive-coloured all over. They were out to enjoy themselves and hated the work. I wanted to enjoy myself too, but up at Schwarzsee it was much easier to do that if you worked hard, than if you appeared sullen and unhappy; Frau Huber responded only to happiness. Her motherly instinct came to the fore then and she basked in the pride of creating a happy family atmosphere—at least on the surface of things.

Days off were hard to come by at Schwarzsee and the weeks would quickly slip by with only promises of such if you appeared to Frau Huber not to be enjoying your work. On the other hand, if you seemed happy and to love the mountains then she would always make time so that you could undertake some special excursion.

The buffet was really my main place of work and after lunch each day that is where I was to be found, ladling spaghetti onto hot plates, cutting thick slices of fruit flan, pouring out liqueurs and apfelsafts and an unending number of coffees, and always struggling to guess the language of the next person in the queue and with what currency he would pay. There was never a shortage of customers.

At lunchtime there was a two-hour halt in the cable car traffic, so that most of the people who had come up during the morning were faced with the choice of eating at Schwarzsee before returning on the first cable car after lunch or going without. Even those choosing to walk back would usually decide to eat first. We were fortunate, therefore, in having a captive market. The cable car conductors that were left at Schwarzsee over the lunch period always ate with us and there were also a fair number of Italian workmen that used to materialise for the lunchtime drink-up. Some of these were working on various building jobs connected with additional ski runs and cable car stations. These men together with the cable car men always took front position at the table lying immediately in front of the buffet and it was their main lunchtime amusement to watch the buffet helps, as we were known, cope with the queues of hungry visitors. Their jokes were often coarse and I think it was a good thing that I did not understand much that was said. There was fortunately usually one amongst them who acted as a general dampener for the too high-spirited. When the cable car men were absent our links with the outside world were gone, for they acted as postmen and shoppers and without their familiar faces life would sometimes have been very difficult, and also very dull.

Halfway through the season, all we younger girls on the buffet were given turquoise blue smocks to wear. This was a new innovation and the sight of Heidi, Peppita and I all lined up behind the buffet at lunchtime with these voluminous smocks enveloping whatever shape we had was too much to resist. Hans, a blonde, bucolic mid-thirties man who was the chief joker amongst the cable car men just stood in the doorway of the hotel the first morning that he saw us and shook his head sadly at Frau Huber.

"Oh this is dreadful," he said, "all these young girls pregnant so soon." Frau Huber laughed, but I think she was a little hurt that her new idea, with which she had been so pleased, had been so ridiculed. I loved my smock nevertheless; it was cool and gay and kept my own clothes clean and there was nothing of the stiffness about it that goes with the traditional waitress's uniform. I had dreaded that I might have to wear a white blouse and pencil-thin black skirt and those dreadful mini lace aprons that Swiss railway buffet waitresses always seem to wear, where the apron attempts to conceal an enormous purse of money balanced directly on the stomach. I always think there is something slightly obscene in the way they lift their aprons with a quick toss and rummage in their purses for the small change.

The one appeal of the buffet to the customer was its cheap meals, for in Switzerland, and in Zermatt where eating out is not cheap, many of the guests found it a welcome change to be able to order sausage and potato salad and pay perhaps only five francs for their lunch instead of the usual set lunch price of about ten francs plus 10 percent. A fair price was something that appealed to Schwarzsee's guests since many were students and young climbers, and most were individual travellers who had to count their pockets instead of benefit from group reductions. Schwarzsee was really a staging post on the route to the Matterhorn in summer and young men in groups and with their guides formed a solid part of the clientele.

In addition, the walking excursion to Schwarzsee from Zermatt was a very popular one despite the fact that it took about three hours if you were not too fit and involved very steep gradients to cover a rise in altitude of over three thousand feet. Such a walk had a very good effect on the buffet sales of drinks and fodder.

The Zermatters themselves were great patrons of the hotel, particularly the guides, who would always join the table with the cable car men. Soon I knew many of them by name and sight, a necessity when I discovered that they paid special rates at the buffet. There were two price lists, one for regular clients and one marked "Arbeiter," the honourable German word for worker. The prices on the second list were at least a third less. I remember on my first day charging two guides the full price and finding out only later. Neither of them had queried the price I had charged them, knowing that I was new, but afterwards I always took great care to make sure that I picked the right list for the right person. One could not afford to alienate the locals. Of course, it was not always very easy to tell who they were. There was one very grubby old man with bad teeth and decayed clothes who brought Frau Huber rushing with smiles when he appeared.

"Who on earth is that?" I asked Heidi, as we stood together in a slack period passing our opinions in monotones on the guests that were scattered about the restaurant.

"That is Herr Otler from the village."

"But why should he be so popular? He doesn't look as though he is well off."

"Now that's where you just can't judge the Swiss by external appearances. He is in fact one of the biggest and richest builders in Zermatt." I looked again at the old man with renewed interest and found he was looking equally intently at me. I found him repulsive, but unfortunately at that moment Frau Huber came towards me bringing Herr Otler with her.

"Virginia, here is someone who wants to meet you. This is the little English girl that I was telling you about. Look how the mountain air is bringing colour to her cheeks. She was so pale when she came you know, but now in Switzerland, she looks just like a rose..." This was the sort of introduction that Frau Huber was very fond of giving where I was concerned, and the fact that I stood five foot six in my stocking feet and had always been considered well built did not deter her in the least from always describing me as small. Neither did I ever understand where she had first discovered the idea that I was so pale on arrival because at that time I lived in Brighton and had always been what is cheerfully known as a healthy looking girl by the older generation.

"Guten Morgen Fraulein." Herr Otler extended his hand across the counter and leered toothily at me. He was, if anything, even more repulsive close to than at a distance.

"Was möchten Sie?" I asked, practising my new German phrases on him, trying to turn the whole thing into a businesslike situation, and he ordered Café Kirsch. This was the favourite drink of the Swiss, black coffee with a glass of their most famous liqueur, made from cherries. They would pour the Kirsch straight into the coffee and drink it in one gulp. You could get pretty drunk very quickly if you were not used to drinking it, as I found to my cost on a couple of occasions. Herr Otler's breath was already well spiced with what must have been four or five similar tipples during the course of the day.

"Was kostet das?"

"Is he an Arbeiter?" I quickly nudged Heidi, and she nodded. His coffee was only eighty centimes but he thrust a ten-franc note at me. I gave him the change and as I did so he pulled my hand back and stuffed the change into my palm.

"That is for you," he said.

"But I am not allowed to."

"Take it or I will give it to Peppita." I took it immediately, feeling very embarrassed and rather like a courtesan being paid in expectation. From my first day I had been told that we must not accept tips on the self-service buffet, and that if anybody should insist on tipping then it should go into a communal cup on the shelf behind. Frau Huber signalled me to take it and then drifted away with him. Later Heidi told me that Herr Otler had jokingly told Frau Huber that he would pay one hundred francs if he could have the opportunity to sleep with the young virgin that he presumed me to be. Somehow I did not feel flattered to hear of this semi-joke, but it goes without saying that I never gave him the chance to put his joke into practice. He came up to Schwarzsee many times and always played the same trick when he bought his coffees, but I usually tried to avoid serving him, leaving the two Austrians, if they happened to be there, to compete for the grandiose tip. Financially, a nine-franc tip from one customer was a reasonable reward for pouring out one coffee.

Tipping was quite a problem. Self-service was something new at that time in Switzerland and the tipping habit dies hard. The time spent in telling someone it was not necessary to tip was really better spent in pocketing the small change before Frau Huber appeared around the corner. The communal cup was nearly always empty so I presumed that the other buffet workers must have done the same thing as myself. Working on the buffet could, therefore, turn out to be a fairly profitable business. We were, of course, paid a standard wage and were fed and kept free, and so the tips that one made from the buffet, as well as from any guests that stayed a fair amount of time, made working up at Schwarzsee a rewarding adventure.

I never managed to store my earnings, however, because of the variety of trips and excursions that I took whilst working there. The Italian families must have accrued large amounts since they never went outside the hotel bounds when they were off duty. Guido and his wife Pasqualina usually spent such time sitting about ten yards away from the terrace with arms round each others waist and a rather expensive transistor radio held up to Guido's ear. I doubt if he could have heard much on it because the reception at that altitude was notoriously bad. The other couple, Valentino and Italia, did little more than stroll leisurely up and down by the hotel entrance, passing casual comment to those that worked on. I could not understand why they did not go down to Zermatt, for as workers, we paid much-reduced rates on the cable cars, but they seemed totally unaware of their surroundings, impervious to the scenery and uninterested in exploration. They were peasant Italians earning their livelihood and nothing else was of interest to them. They spoke only Italian and Frau Huber found difficulty in making them understand her, often because they chose to misunderstand more than anything else. The two wives were giggly, gentle, and both pregnant by a few months, but their husbands were made of harder material. Guido was a squat, phlegmatic person until roused—and that took some effort, but Valentino was an awkward person indeed and unfortunately the sort that gave Italian workers in Switzerland the bad reputation that they seemed to collect. He was reasonably good-looking but ignorant and arrogant and he objected strongly to any form of correction. He and Frau Huber were tailor-made to argue and row they often did. The usual time was early evening when the stone floor of the buffet was regularly washed and cleaned. This activity always seemed to be the trigger for Frau Huber to complain and Valentino to shout. He was insolent and rough but it was difficult not to be amused by the manner in which Frau Huber would lose her temper, because her voice always reached a high pitch that defied any sort of imitation and her few Italian words became hopelessly intermingled with other languages and inevitably she finished by shouting in English or French and so becoming totally incomprehensible to the Italians. Before the end of the season Valentino and his wife had to leave because of his attempts to sabotage the water supply by leaving taps running throughout the hotel and using other such methods. The supply was very limited at Schwarzsee since it had to be pumped uphill and stored in a small tank and Valentino's efforts came near to ruining the last month of the hotel's season.

There had been trouble throughout the summer with thieving, particularly of food, and Frau Huber, with the support of Heidi—who was very much involved in finances—undertook numerous methods to safeguard the supplies, but it was never wholly possible to lock up everything. Most of the perishable foods were kept in huge cool rooms leading off the kitchen and the rest of the supplies were stored down in the cellar. Every evening the buffet was emptied of all but the bottles of wines and soft drinks and it was my task first thing in the morning to unlock the buffet and kitchen doors and open up the great kitchen refrigerators. Sometimes hunks of cheese were missing, sometimes *wurst*, but more often than not, slices of huge flat fruit flans. These were both the easiest and the most tasty things to steal since they could be eaten cold and on their own. They were unfortunately Frau Huber's favourite dish because she had a very sweet tooth. She, therefore, took particularly unkindly to the disappearance of these tasty flans.

The flans were about ten inches in diameter with a soft crust around the edge that crumbled at a touch. They had delicious fillings of strawberries or peaches or whatever other fruit was available. I used to enjoy the afternoons that Frau Huber worked with me on the buffet because her favourite pastime was to finger these flans, slicing them and tidying them into shape with her fingers until the crusts eventually fell apart.

"Tut tut, Virginia, come a moment, are you feeling hungry?" Of course, I always nodded to that question. "Well you can eat this if you like. It is no good to sell like that now that the crust has broken." I needed no second bidding but disappeared into the kitchen to gobble it down, because it was most unseemly to be seen eating on the buffet. Whilst I was away Frau Huber was slowly knocking another piece of flan into a similar un-saleable morsel for herself.

In fact there was no need at all to steal food at Schwarzsee because the meals for the staff were both many and plentiful, and Frau Huber could rarely refuse a request for more. Following lunch at about eleven, there was tea of bread and jam in the midafternoon and supper at six. I did not see what Valentino, if it was he, could have gained by stealing, other than perhaps the feeling of successfully venting his spite at the country from which he was forced to gain a livelihood and which kept him so far from his own home and background.

Another rather different case of theft occurred with the young Italian Carlo, who left the hotel after I had been there only about a fortnight, and who disappeared ignominiously to Zermatt with a great suitcase and tears freely flowing. I never knew the full story behind his sudden departure, but it could not have been too criminal because he stayed on in Zermatt and obtained another job in a hotel in the village. Had she wished, Frau Huber could have insisted on his leaving Switzerland, because every foreigner working in Switzerland is carefully watched and checked and all passports are held in the local police station for the duration of the work period. With a black record with the police and your passport in custody it was difficult indeed to obtain further employment if you had once been troublesome.

At the time I was sorry to see Carlo leave because he was the only young man on the staff, and certainly the only male who seemed interested in females. On reflection, however, it was probably better that he departed when he did because an amorous Italian under the same roof for a period of months would have needed stronger resistance than I possessed. He was attractive in a typical full-lipped, sensual manner, and the evening entertainment at Schwarzsee was somewhat limited in range and diversity. Carlo was the same age as I and very dark and well built. He came from the north of Italy and was far more educated than the two Italian couples. He was at an experimental period of his life, like myself, but whereas I was out to find out about everything in general, he had only one interest in particular: sex, and how his sex appeal rated in the general market. The only time that I really came into contact with him in a work capacity was on the buffet, for it was his job to bring up the crates of soft drinks and wines from the cellar and keep us well supplied.

"Peppita, I need some more Orangina and Sinalco and Coca Cola," I called one busy lunch hour.

"Call Carlo then." Peppita's gold tooth flashed from the further end of the buffet as she continued pouring out a dozen coffees in a matter of seconds.

"Carlo!" I stuck my head into the kitchen and shouted. I need not have bothered to shout. His head almost touched mine from the other side of the small connecting hatch. "Bottles—I need some more Coca Cola, Sinalco and Orangina, now." I was desperate, for the queue was building up towards the door and a large group of American soft-drink addicts had just emptied out of the last cable car.

A wide grin spread across Carlo's face and he blew a kiss at me through the hatch, before departing at a leisurely pace towards the cellar.

"Where's the Coke?" A pushy, plimsolled American scholar with glasses stood on the other side of the counter.

"You'll have to wait a moment, I'm afraid, for some more supplies to come up."

"Well haven't you got any cold milk then?"

"Yes we have. Do you want a glass?"

"Oh no, I'll wait for the Coke." The young American stood blocking up the buffet counter talking and generally showing off his enquiring mind. Carlo arrived a moment later bringing only the Orangina with him. It took three more trips before the Coca Cola finally appeared and by then I was faced with about twenty irate customers, pushing from the back, all eager to get their plate-loads of half-cooked Swiss sausages with potato salad, and furious at the hold-up.

It was on these occasions that Carlo's romantic ardour was the most irritating. He would insist on unloading the crates on the buffet instead of leaving them just outside, and spent his time diving in and out between my legs putting the bottles into their correct places in the containers and on the shelves. Every time that I bent down to get another bottle he was right behind, and whenever I turned around I could not help bumping into him because the buffet was too narrow to allow two people to stand side by side.

Carlo's loss to the hotel was all in all not a great one, and as the season got underway the large number of young climbers and campers who spent their evenings drinking and dining in the hotel soon filled up any gap in pleasant male company that was left by his departure.

There was one Italian in the hotel who bore no relation to the other Italian workers either in class or education and that was Maria, the waitress of the silver-service restaurant and my roommate.

Maria Salvatore was a slim, articulate woman from the province of Belluno in the Italian Dolomites. She came to Schwarzsee four days after myself, and as I watched her arrival off the cable car and stately journey over to the hotel, all fears that I might not like my prospective roommate were dispelled.

She walked straight-backed and light-footed across the tough ground, her shoulder-length dark hair neatly turned under and held in control by a headband. Her suitcase was carried by Johann, a local Swiss who spent much of his time at Schwarzsee running the other cable car station that went down to Furgg, and which was a few years later to provide the link for a second cable car route to Zermatt. I was washing my hair at the time, in the two hours that I had free most afternoons, and was perched on the windowsill trying to dry it in the hot sun before returning to work. Maria's arrival rendered such uncomfortable manoeuvres unnecessary. A few minutes after I watched her step inside the hotel entrance she appeared in the bedroom doorway, led by Heidi and my days of making do were over. Maria was a model of what an itinerant hotel worker should be. Within minutes of starting to unpack her belongings she had produced every conceivable gadget for comfortable living that it was possible to transport in one suitcase. Needless to say, a hair dryer was just one of these items and I secretly congratulated myself on the life of luxury to which I could now look forward.

I watched her sensible clothes so correct for mountain living being lifted carefully out of their wrappings and squashed my own meagre collection of unsuitable summer dresses as far into the corner of the wardrobe as possible to make room for Maria's.

"You will have to use French, Virginia, as your common language," said Heidi as she departed. I was delighted at such an opportunity and also surprised, since no Italian I had yet met spoke anything other than his native tongue.

"So you can speak French," I smiled at Maria, speaking in French, which became our common language.

"Oh yes," she replied, busying herself around the small room. "I worked with a French family for a year in Paris, and learnt most of my French then."

"That explains your perfect accent."

"Oh no, I am not perfect at all," she shrugged off my praise. "I am afraid that my German is much better than my French, since where I come from in Italy, a lot of German is spoken because of the historical links with Austria." I thought that was rather a polite way of describing Italy's subjugation to the Habsburgs but said no more. I was beginning to feel one degree under in the presence of this super-waitress.

Her manners were exquisite, her courtesy almost overwhelming. There was hardly room for the two of us to move about in the bedroom at the same time and occasionally when we collided both our apologies hung confused in the air.

"Are you fond of mountains?" I just had to ask my favourite question.

"Oh yes, I live in the mountains. It is only a small village in the Dolomites, very isolated in the wintertime and sometimes I must ski long distances across the valleys to visit my friends in the neighbouring villages." Her eyes became clouded as she talked of her native village and she drew some photographs from a small wallet.

"That is my mother and father in front of our house," I looked at a solid couple of elderly mountain folk, "And here I am with my sister last winter." Maria was smiling out from the photograph against a fairytale background of snow and mountains, with skis balanced nonchalantly against her shoulder. I was envious. Zermatt and Schwarzsee obviously could not seem as unique to Maria as they did to me. She was accustomed to to wake up and find Alpine sunrises and glistening cold mornings and sleepy mountain valleys just outside her bedroom window, and yet she was outwardly more civilized than any South Kensington debutante and far more self-controlled than myself. She was ten years older than I was and unmarried.

"I have not yet found the perfect man," she explained that first evening when we became more confidential as we tucked down to sleep. I found it easier to ask these sort of intimate questions when the room was dark, and I could pretend that I had known Maria longer than just a few hours.

"But is there such as thing?"

"For me there is. You see he must have this certain quality about him. How can I describe it?" She thought for a moment. "I'm sorry but I think that I can only describe it by using an Italian word to explain what I mean. He must be *sympatico*, you understand me?"

"I think so." I tried to think of any of the male hotel staff qualifying under Maria's scrutiny for this label. The task was a difficult one. Certainly the chef was out, and Carlo, who had not yet left the hotel when Maria arrived, was too young by her standards. Maria, of course, did not eat with the other Italians in the basement, but was classified with group one. At supper on her first evening Maria and Peppita obviously liked each other very much and since Peppita spoke fluent Italian, partly owing to a longstanding romantic liaison on Lake Como, animated conversation had developed between them that was only the precursor of many more. They were both of an age, both unmarried, both virtuous, if that is the right word to use, and both very fond of discussing love, marriage, and men in theory. I was a witness to their conversation on this and on many more occasions, and a rather poor witness I made since I understood little more than one word in twenty and perhaps only half the gestures that accompanied the words. Nevertheless, I loved to sit and listen to them talking in the evenings. The pleasure of hearing the Italian language was in no way diminished by my lack of comprehension. I think that I perhaps came away with a far more elevated feeling from their conversations than they did themselves, and saved myself the trouble of participation. I was petted and spoiled by them both since to them I was still only a girl, and without prior approval, they and Maria in particular set themselves up as the custodians of my virtue whilst I was at Schwarzsee, something that I found rather amusing in theory, but somewhat irritating when an attempt was made to put it into practice. The combination of motherly Frau Huber and watchdog Maria could have made my stay a very safe one indeed, but as the season wore on and Maria became busier working late in the restaurant, and Frau Huber more anxious checking over the receipts in the office late into each night, I found myself more free to indulge in a few harmless flirtations across the buffet. Poor Heidi, who many times would have liked to join me in chatting to some young climbers who were staying overnight in the hotel, was invariably locked away with Frau Huber, typing furiously into the small hours of the morning.

With Maria's arrival at Schwarzsee and that of Gherda and Gherlinda within a days, the complement of staff was complete, and just in time before the summer season became fully flourishing and the whirl of activity unending.

5

❧❧❧❀❧❧❧

Afternoons brought a lull in the work cycle of the hotel and the siesta period of rest and relaxation. For me, however, the few hours of freedom from work known as *Zimmerstunde* were precious daylight hours for exploration, and there was nothing of the sleepy siesta attitude about my way of behaving when the clock struck 2 pm—freedom hour.

A quick nod from Frau Huber and I was a vanishing apparition, gone up the staircase in two bounds, stripped of my overall in a third, and coated in sun oil before a fourth bound could stop me. Within seconds of release I was back in the buffet, parading in "civvies" and for just a short period of time a lounger with those that I had spent a hot lunch hour envying, those visitors who lolled gently for hours on the sun terrace with their backs to the brickwork and their bodies turning slowly golden. The sort of suntan they would need a week to get on the Riviera they could get in only a few hours at the rarefied mountain heights. They removed themselves from the dazzling, packed terrace for only the short space of time that it took to queue at the counter and obtain what sustenance they needed. I suppose it was unreasonable of me to feel envy when they perhaps had only a few days of a short holiday in which to savour every moment, whereas I was there for the whole summer, but on those days when the sun was high in the sky it was a hateful truth that I begrudged every second of my free time that was not spent outside the hotel itself, indulging in mountain sunlight.

I left my bedroom in a whirlpool of chaos, much to meticulous Maria's consternation, and for a few hours my working disguise fell away. I became a stranger free to wander the little world around the hotel, to stare endlessly at the views and to slip and slide on the treacherous paths, still clogged here and there with patches of unmelted snow.

One of my favourite walks was down to the Schwarzsee itself, the small black lake that lay smooth and quiet in the hollow of the Hörnli outcrop. It was only a few minutes' walk from the hotel but it was entirely hidden from its view. I could sink onto the grass of the steep sloping mountainsides that descended sharply into the water and just dream. On the edge of the lake stood the diminutive whitewashed chapel of Maria zum Schnee, idyllic and isolated in its position, with only the mountain sheep for its permanent parishioners. The lake was so still and smooth that never a ripple disturbed the placid reflection of the chapel in its waters. As a backdrop to the lake and chapel, looking northwards in the direction of Zermatt, were the Dent Blanche, the Obergabelhorn, and the beautiful Weisshorn, another group of the great four-thousand-metre peaks that ring the Zermatt valley.

The Schwarzsee was ice cold, a by-product of the winter snow, made beautiful only by its reflections. I once heard that a Zermatt guide from the village, at the turn of the last century, was returning from climbing the Matterhorn, when he saw a tourist swimming in the lake. He was so frightened by the sight that he nearly collapsed and died. He had never seen anyone swimming before, and the shock of seeing this nude bather, isolated in the centre of the Schwarzsee splashing happily was something he took a while to recover from.

A single service was usually held in the chapel on Sundays, conducted by an itinerant priest for the benefit of the hotel workers and any guests or mountaineers that may have strayed that way. The Italians in our hotel always went to Mass, which was spoken with a thick Swiss-German accent by a priest with his mountain boots protruding beneath his cassock.

On one or two Sundays I managed to persuade Frau Huber to give me enough time off work to attend the service, hoping to leave her confused as to the differences between being an Anglo-Catholic and a Roman Catholic. To me denominational differences were immaterial in such a setting, where the materials of the building itself seemed to provide all the spiritual teaching that was necessary. Frau Huber, however, was not long in discovering that I was a daughter of the Reformation. She stopped my trips with Maria, seeing in them only an attempt to avoid work for an odd hour. After that, my visits to the chapel remained solitary and taken mid afternoon, as a way of escaping from the hurly burly of the flow of guests. The old whitewashed walls, miniature alter and

lack of ornament made the little chapel of Mary of the Snows as ecumenical in its welcome to all that came as anyone could wish. In the last century it must often have served as a place of refuge for mountaineers retreating from the vagaries of the weather on the

Matterhorn, and it was within the chapel that Edward Whymper had stored part of his climbing equipment the day before his successful assault of the Matterhorn on 14th July, 1865. When I was at Schwarzsee, campers often used its small stone porch as a temporary place of refuge on wet and windy afternoons, for the protected hollow in which the lake and chapel were situated was one of the few good camping sites in existence at that altitude around Zermatt. The proximity of the hotel with its facilities further increased its convenience. Despite this, however, I never saw more than the occasional tent and that usually belonged to young hardened English climbers.

At that altitude, nights were very cold and the steep mountain slopes afforded little protection from the wind. Neither were campers made very welcome in the hotel, for their tendency was to stay drinking beer for an entire evening whilst talking to the female staff and Frau Huber saw little profit in that, either for the hotel or for the staff. There was a small group of potholers from the Midlands who camped by Schwarzsee for about two weeks while waiting to attempt the Matterhorn climb. Their welcome became distinctly frosty as the days went on and their evenings in the buffet lengthened into card playing, beer drinking, and chat sessions with myself, Gherda and Gherlinda.

There was a small outhouse or ski cabin connected to the hotel, in which dormitory-type sleeping accommodation was provided for only a few francs a night. Campers were unpopular for depriving the hotel of the income derived from this building.

Personally, I preferred to find no campers around when I walked to the lake, because the small red flapping tents were an intrusion on the solitude of the place. To me, the only rightful tenants of the land were the sheep, and after a while I was glad to find that they equally accepted me.

These mountain sheep were the most inquisitive of animals— large, longhaired, and shaggy, with sweeping curled horns and jangling bells around their necks. It was impossible to visit the lake, particularly in the early evening, without

finding a group of wandering gourmets picking their way amongst the short grass and flowers, seeking out food from the generally stony and unpromising ground. A great favourite with the sheep was Lucas, the young Swiss boy working in the hotel, and together he and I often encouraged them towards the hotel in the evenings with tempting gifts of hard hunks of stale bread. Having got them interested in the hotel, however, the main trouble then was to lose them, as nudging and pushing, they would follow Lucas across the wooden terrace, knocking chairs and tables askew with their unwieldy horns. One particularly large sheep which could be identified individually, if only by her excessively pushy nature, always tried to enter the hotel building in the evenings, but try as she might, at whatever angle she placed her head, the span of her horns was just too wide to fit through the door. She had to remain perched on the steps outside gazing through the entrance, confused and lost.

The sheep were the only form of life that I saw up at Schwarzsee. It was too high there for cattle and for most birds. Once I did hear a piercing whistle which must have belonged to a marmot, but search as often as I did, I never managed to catch sight of these furry animals that burrow and hide on the rough mountainsides.

Despite the rough terrain and stony ground, flowers grew in abundance around the lake and along the mule paths that climbed up and around its shores on towards the Hörnli. Violets, forget-me-nots and all variety of gentian flourished and swayed in the stubby grass, replacing the snow as fast as it melted and providing a gentle covering for an otherwise tough landscape. The tender stems of the violets and blue gentians appeared so incongruous against such a wild background, as they flourished beneath the thick boots of the climbing parties that passed over them in search of greater conquests. Only a few hundred feet above Schwarzsee the flowers ceased to grow altogether and nothing was left but the rocks and stones that formed the enormous solid base of the Matterhorn. Once, I found a small clump of Edelweiss hiding in a crag at about nine thousand feet, but when I tried to find the same spot a second time I failed. I only hope that no one had picked the flowers in the meantime for they are protected in Switzerland, and my interest had been only in the finding, not the picking.

Heidi was my usual companion on these afternoon excursions since Frau Huber seemed pleased to arrange it so that our free hours coincided. Heidi was very valuable to her as a competent linguist and even more importantly as a competent hotel secretary who was prepared to work all hours into the night. By providing Heidi with a companion, Frau Huber hoped to keep her a little more content throughout the summer. I was pleased with the arrangement since I soon discovered that Heidi was easy company, someone who enjoyed acting on another's initiative, and I was always ready to provide that initiative. I never found a problem in thinking up a promising excursion in the neighbourhood, and then suggesting it to Heidi. She would become easily dazzled by the thought, and since she had the ear of Frau Huber, within no time at all the two of us were away, climbing over the boulders and jumping amongst the abandoned ski runs of the mountain slopes. Sometimes we even managed to escape for an hour or so to Zermatt. It was very difficult to reach Zermatt within the two hour *Zimmerstunde* since the cable cars only ran every twenty minutes. There was a change at Furi onto a second car, and then a half-mile walk from the terminus station into Zermatt itself. We sometimes managed, if the timing was just right, and raced from shop to shop on errands for others as well as for ourselves, often returning with a great mound of cherries that dyed our lips red. As workers we had special coupons for the journey but, if we were lucky, a favourite cable car man might be on duty and we could save those coveted coupons for another trip when our luck was not so favourable.

It was surprising how little I missed the shops whilst at Schwarzsee and the civilization that they bring in their wake. The few urgent items that I needed were usually purchased for me by Johann or one of the other regular cable car drivers at the hotel, and they never let me down. I remember, however, on one occasion urgently wanting a lipstick and begging Johann to buy me one in the village chemist. The hotel had been far too busy for me to be able to escape, and offers to run messages from Frau Huber had fallen on deaf ears. Johann undertook the errand but the next morning I was called to the telephone. His voice was worried.

"Virginia, I am in the chemist now and they ask me what make do you want?"

"Anything will do as long as it is not too expensive."

I should have known better than to make that qualification, for in the Zermatt shops everything is always the most expensive.

"But what sort of colour do you want?"

"A kind of light pinky-orange."

His voice faded away with anxiety at the other end as he repeated my request to the shop assistant.

"She says that they have pink but that it has no orange colour in it."

It was all becoming far too complicated, but Johann was determined to complete his mission successfully and the conversation dragged on through colour range, translation and incomprehension for nearly five minutes. I trembled as I saw him coming into the hotel at lunchtime. I steeled myself to thank him enormously for whatever he appeared with, and managed with some measure of success to convince him at least. The only trouble was, of course, that I was forced to wear a brilliant orange lipstick for the rest of my stay in honour of his kindness.

Maria was not pleased with Frau Huber's attempts to turn me into Heidi's companion, since she had obviously hoped to mould me as her own, despite the fact that she spent the best part of most days talking with Peppita about their past loves and lives and their future aspirations. Maria loved to have someone younger and impressionable whom she could influence and dominate. She was the born older sister, a frustrated mother. It was irritating for her to feel that I was perhaps not as easily controllable as she had first thought. We shared a room together but Frau Huber was always suggesting, at Heidi's instigation, that I should change over and share with the latter. The atmosphere was almost that of a girl's hall of residence but for the preponderance of males amongst the guests and their easy fraternization with the staff.

Maria was always so good at whatever she undertook that I was forced to listen to her advice. She had been in hotels most of her working life and had a grasp of their machinations that made her my natural tutor. In addition, her knowledge of mountain life and the ease and grace with which she seemed always to be dressed correctly for the elemental changes further increased her superiority, in my eyes at least. But it was in the restaurant that her superiority really shone forth, and particularly on those crowded days when I was called from the buffet to help her.

It was Maria's world amongst the starched white tablecloths, as she stood slim and neat in her black and white uniform with a fixed smile of welcome for all who crossed the threshold, and a slight uncomprehending glaze of the eyes when she could not understand the language of the visitors.

A restaurant always takes its formality from the staff and at Schwarzsee it was no exception. The silver-service waitressing and the pageantry of serving and being served were worthy of the London Savoy, regardless of the incongruous dress of the guests, often hot and dishevelled from a glut of physical exercise, and the noise and hurly burly issuing from the self-service buffet. I have to admit that the only days when the tone was slightly lowered were the days that I was promoted to assist. I was terrified by the necessity to learn how to serve vegetables balanced delicately between two spoons and to pour wine over the back of the hand so that no telltale stain of red gradually crept across the white surface of the tablecloth. I am left-handed and always managed to pop up on the wrong side of every guest. As they leant to the left to allow me room to serve I appeared on the left and collision was the automatic conclusion. On the buffet the essence of the job was speed and speed alone. In the restaurant speed was required indeed, but a speed that was mute and camouflaged. The swing doors rocked to and fro as Maria sped, as though on air, from kitchen to table and back again, ignoring the shouts from the chef and the insults that he hurled into the void more for effect than with any particular malice. I stumbled and struggled and smiled and fortunately gained many sympathetic smiles in return.

On one particular day, however, a group of French visitors were seated waiting to eat. On each day there was a table d'hôte menu, which allowed for a choice between four different meals. Each meal was numbered and guests selected the number. My group of five selected menu number four and a few minutes later I proudly bore in five plates of steaming Schublig with roast potatoes. Their faces expressed absolute horror as they gazed at the large semicooked sausages lying on their plates.

"But we did not order these."

"Oh yes, you ordered number four."

I fetched over the menu for the day and pointed out to them the choice they had made.

"But I am sure that that is not what was written on our menu," said the leader of the group, his hand shaking with anger as he stretched it out to show me what was written on the menu I had given to them when they first entered the restaurant. My stomach turned as I looked closely at it. The menu I had given him was for the previous day, when number four had been a delicious meal of steak cooked in mushroom sauce. I blanched as Maria and Frau Huber closed in upon the scene. One certain fact was that there was no steak on today's menu and somebody was going to have to eat those half-cooked sausages. Nobody was going to have steak. With noble reticence and forbearing the five guests attacked the plates that were in front of them, conscious that at least they had been granted a reduction in the overall price of the meal. I took a very wide course round their table until I saw them safely walking in the direction of the hotel exit.

Maria was not paid a standard salary but depended in the main on the 10 percent service charge that was automatically added to every bill. In addition, she also took the small tips that guests felt obliged to leave despite the service charge that was already included in the price. It is surprising how few people have strength of character enough to leave a restaurant after a full meal without leaving the sprinkling of loose change shining obviously on the tablecloth or the waiting plate. In most cases none of the guests who came to eat at Schwarzsee would ever be returning and yet none were quite brave enough to retreat with a hostile silence and the classification of "mean" piercing their backs as they exited. I must admit that I always leave a tip regardless and get quite a nice sensation as a result, a sort of feeling of being loved and of thinking how the staff must classify me as a pleasant guest. I am not sure who benefits the most from this feeling but I would much rather feel like that than make for the door with the speed of a pistol shot and my eyes forced forward for fear of what I might see behind me. Of course, the people who can manage to walk away without leaving a thing are always the ones that feel no sense of embarrassment whatsoever, the "tough-as-boots" brigade.

At Schwarzsee I looked especially brightly on the generous tippers when I helped Maria, since I did not take any of the service charge, only the crumbs that were left behind and that Maria was kind enough to throw my way.

Maria was a most calculating worker who made a considerable amount of money out of her time spent in hotels. By working in the smaller hotels she probably worked harder and had less time off because there was only herself in charge, but it also meant that a much greater share of the profits came her way. On several occasions at Schwarzsee when large and important events took place, like a special feast or a wedding meal, professional waiters were brought up from Zermatt to help and they were not satisfied with just taking the small change. They were on an equal basis, and Maria saw the crowded restaurant split three ways. For her it was much better to make do with a little amateur help in the shape of someone like myself.

At night when she finished in the restaurant, often late by the time the last guests had savoured their endless cups of conversational coffee, she would sit up in bed counting and marking down in a small black book the takings of the day. I was usually reading or talking but nothing ever distracted her from the necessity of getting, and keeping, her accounts in order.

"It is so important to keep a check every day, otherwise I may forget." I always thought that was rather an unlikely event. Her hair rollers bobbed and shook as she counted and sorted the cash and stored it away in her wallet, in the suitcase beneath the bed.

"What are you saving for Maria?" I asked her one night.

She hesitated a moment.

"For when I get married. It is important that a woman should have some of her own money. It means that you can have more of the things that you really want around you."

"Have you ever met anyone that you felt like marrying?"

"No, not yet." She smiled a rather secret smile.

"But what about that Italian climber that was in the hotel the other night? You seemed to spend a lot of time talking with him, and I heard him say that he is coming back this way, after his climb to Italy."

"We shall see." I was surprised to get so positive a response from her. The climber had been a man in his forties, tall, thickset and quiet. He was alone and had set off from Schwarzsee to traverse the Theodule Pass and descend to Cervinia in Italy. He was due to return our way after spending a few days in his own country and was doing some small climbs en route.

Crossing the Theodul Pass on foot into Italy was a favourite excursion from Schwarzsee, the one snow traverse of the Alps, where it was comparatively easy to break the barrier thrown up by the mountains along the Swiss-Italian border. Apparently during the Second World War the pass had been a favourite escape route from Italy for the Partisans and the Swiss frontier guards had many a time turned their backs on neutrality to help the weary and inexperienced make a successful crossing of the wide snow plain, fraught as it was with concealed crevasses and the unforeseeable dangers of weather changes.

When Maria's climbing friend reappeared, I watched as they exchanged stories whilst she served him in the restaurant. For once her aura of formality slipped slightly, but he left after a night and no more was heard of him. Maria went on earning and saving, and it was not until I had returned to England at the end of the summer that I learnt in her letters of a romance that had been blossoming unseen during the whole of that summer. Maria had become engaged to Johann, the kindly controller of the second cable car route to Schwarzsee who had spent so much of his time helping the ladies of the hotel with their shopping errands, and the man with whom I had first seen her entering the hotel on the day she had arrived. Within a few months they were married in her hometown in the Dolomites and as a result of that first summer season in Zermatt Maria became a permanent resident of the town.

When I returned as a tourist a few years later I visited her in her chalet apartment on the outskirts of the village and it was only then that I saw to what use Maria had put those years of slaving and working. She sat pregnant and resplendent serving tea in most perfectly equipped surroundings that must have cost a prohibitive price, since Zermatt is possibly one of the most expensive places in Switzerland in which to purchase houses and flats. A full-length balcony ran along the apartment facing south towards the Matterhorn and glass-fronted built in wardrobes shone in the bedrooms. Apparent opulence sprang from the walls and I sat in an envious state wondering why I had bothered to go to university only to become an eligible employee in London's smoky business world. I obviously should have trained as a waitress and become fluent in several languages and then I too could have afforded to settle and live in a place that can only remain for me as an idyll. The only thought with which I could satisfy myself that afternoon as I sat delicately drinking tea amongst the rubber plants and fitted carpets of Maria's home was that even the permanent view of the Matterhorn outside one's living room window must eventually become commonplace and therefore lose its magic. In some perverse way I prefer to keep the magic.

All this, however, was unknown and undreamt of as I worked with Maria that summer and watched the variety of guests that came and went.

On occasion, a large group of students came and stayed for an evening and ate in the restaurant. They were on Alpine tours and a night in a mountain hotel was a usual part of the itinerary. This was not always enjoyable for me, for the groups were large and self-sufficient enough not to need my company for the evening entertainment. It was easy to feel excluded by one's own age group and it was not a very pleasant feeling when that occurred. French students were particularly bad for this, with their "in" laughter, jokes and singing that continued late into the night. One evening, when such a group arrived, I stood on the other side of the swing doors leading into the kitchen, peeping through the glass partition—the outsider looking in. I should not have felt that way, and to Maria it was strange that I did, but she was so used to hotel life that to her it was unnatural to join in. In fact she would often look askance at my easy and casual manner with guests, but to me Schwarzsee was a place of informality. Working on the buffet it was difficult to be otherwise, but something did change in the atmosphere in the restaurant as heavy mountain boots passed through the artificial barrier of potted plants to be waited upon, rather than to wait upon themselves. It was the small world of luxury in which Frau Huber enjoyed doing her daily parade, passing to and fro between the tables flashing her Pekinese smile and demanding satisfied thanks in return.

A well-known Italian conductor and his wife stayed a fortnight and never emerged from the bedroom until noon but shouted requests for food and drinks from the bedroom terrace down to the ground floor. One late afternoon a strange silent Englishman in his late forties arrived for two nights and failed to appear at all for the whole of the second day. He had the preoccupied air of a potential suicide and I spent most of the day, at Frau Huber's request, listening in a cramped position at the door of his room. To my utmost relief he appeared at supper that evening still as preoccupied as when he had first arrived at the hotel but obviously none the worse for his quiet day of rest.

These, however, were not typical of the majority of the guests. Our guests were in mountain gear with suntanned features and one interest alone: to sit and gaze at mountain panoramas for as long as the light would allow them. They would be up as early as possible in order not to miss a moment of the morning splendour of the sunrise on the peaks, and to stay outside the hotel walking or climbing for as long as the sun stayed high and the quick-descending mountain mists held off.

All nationalities passed through but I particularly remember the Italians and the Americans, the first for their happiness and the loud exuberance that they brought to the life of the hotel, and the second for their strange analytical approach to enjoyment. The majority of American visitors were students touring Europe prior to returning to the States. The Matterhorn was a must on their itinerary, if only because it was one of the few European mountains with which they had probably been familiar since childhood, because of the large-scale model of the Matterhorn in Disneyland, Los Angeles. They came to see it in reality and as soon as they had, they moved on. More often than not they did not see it at all because the Matterhorn can be a very temperamental mountain that would disappear entirely from view for a whole day. If that day happened to coincide with the only day allotted for viewing in a month's itinerary of Europe then misfortune can strike indeed. However, many of the young Americans that visited Schwarzsee were permanently based in Switzerland studying in the international colleges and schools of Lausanne and Geneva. Zermatt was, for them, a close holiday playground. To this group the Matterhorn was not the prime object of importance. It was rather Zermatt as a ski resort, not a mountain-climbing centre, that they loved and I used to tire of listening to the praises of the winter skiing enthusiasts.

Mountain climbers are far less social than skiers. Perhaps there is less social kudos to talking about climbing than there is to talking about the world of après-ski. For my part I would far rather walk the mule paths of the Alps and trust to my feet than attempt a *schuss* down a vertical drop with elongated appendages strapped insecurely to all my extremities. Neither did I change my opinion after I tried to ski on a later winter holiday in Zermatt. I have no love of speed or height, and you need both to make a successful skier. I suppose it is the same spirit that makes me prefer to drive in a hard-topped saloon than a racy sports car.

There were few occasions when the chance arose for the hotel staff to go out at night, to form a pleasure-seeking group of singing and drinking friends on the lookout for fun and entertainment outside the familiar walls of Schwarzsee Hotel. For such an event to occur a number of factors had to coincide. Maria had to empty the restaurant early by appearing rushed and hasty and Peppita and I had to clear and restock the buffet for the next day in record time. Gherda and Gherlinda must be able to beautify themselves sufficiently after the working day to make themselves ready for a night out and the chef had to find enough time to finish his cursing and skipping exercises at an earlier hour than usual. Added to this, Lucas had to be packed off to bed quickly to avoid the necessity of taking him with us, Frau Huber had to be in an amiable and passive mood, and Heidi had to agree to being sacrificed as the one to stay behind in order to get Frau Huber into just such a state of mind.

One evening all these factors occurred through force and persuasion and six of us stood on the steps of the hotel muffled up to face the cold night and all set to step out into the dark void around in search of adventure. We had to look hard! Below the lights of Zermatt twinkled and shone, the lights that showed the numerous small bars and restaurants that were warm and inviting and waiting for just such a group as ourselves to descend upon them. They would have to wait. Even the stamina of Maria, could not take us that far, when we considered the daunting prospect of walking back to the hotel with a stomach full of wine and legs weak with alcoholic effect and physical exhaustion.

"Where should we go?" had been the cry throughout the day, after the first plan had been laid, and the answer was "to the Stafelalp Hotel," and so it was to Stafelalp that we set off. It involved a descent of over a thousand feet, an hour's walk along a stony path that passed by the chapel and the lake and that then crept around the flanks of the Matterhorn until descending directly beneath its great northern wall. The path took us away from Zermatt and in the direction of the Schonbiel Hut and the Dent D'Herens, a beautiful mountain in its own right but which seemed only a smaller version of the Matterhorn, or its insignificant echo when viewed from the Zermatt valley.

The descent was not as steep as the usual route down from Schwarzsee to Zermatt, which dropped directly in front of the hotel, but it was steep enough at night with a group of people. We continually slipped and stubbed our feet on the pebbles, invisible in the darkness. The mountains were great overhanging shadows. The Zmutt Glacier at the base of the Matterhorn floated in cracked ice and rock formation, a massive wall between us and the mountain. There was total silence broken only by our breathing and the whoops of Herr Hausmann plunging suddenly madly downwards in quick bursts of energy aimed at frightening us all into fearing for his safety. At one moment he disappeared over a small dip in the path ahead and we gasped and rushed forward expecting to see a great chasm opening up with his body invisible at the bottom, but the path only continued in undulating manner and Herr Hausmann laughed happily at the success of his small joke.

At one point I dropped behind, intent on trying to catch the silence for just a moment. Within seconds the dark night had swallowed them up and I stood breathing the cold air and feeling the sting of the night wind on my face. My eyes had grown accustomed to the dark and I could pick out the silhouettes of the mountains across the valley. A sudden soft warmth brushed my legs. I went to scream but no noise emerged. I looked down and found a large sheep busy examining my boots. She had found me in the dark, a stationary object in her territory that obviously aroused her curiosity. I bent down and fondled the great curling horns and felt the thick coat of wool that protected her from feeling the wind that was beginning to circulate freely beneath my sweater and I envied her the right to be there and her freedom to roam so casually amongst the boulders and to creep up so noiselessly upon an intruder. She soon tired of my affectionate embraces and ambled silently away and I started to run to catch up with the others. Without my friendly sheep beside me I suddenly felt very lonely and in need of the protection of my temporary family group.

We descended below the treeline and found ourselves no longer exposed to the wind but protected by the slowly thickening forest, and our steps became brisker.

We had been walking for about forty-five minutes when we came upon the Stafelalp Hotel, a small mountain inn nestled amongst the trees just off to the side of the pathway and almost invisible in the dark. We came to a halt at the steps leading up to its entrance. It looked closed. Surely we had not come all that way for nothing?

Maria and I climbed the stairs and pushed the door open. It gave at a touch, and we walked into the dark passage and knocked on the first door that we came to.

"Herein!"

Maria and I peered round the doorway into a long, partially lit room. A heavy wooden table ran down its centre. Seated at the furthest end were three men, only their faces and full glasses visible in the light of two spluttering candles.

"What do you want?"

"Is the hotel open?"

A guffaw ran round the table at the word hotel.

"It is never closed to young ladies." Another ribald laugh.

"But is it possible to get something to drink? We have come from the Schwarzsee; we work there," said Maria, spelling it out for them.

Immediately the attitude of the three changed. The owner stood up and shook hands. "How many of there are you? Do you want wine? Two bottles of Fendant? I'll get some more candles." He apologized for the welcome. "We don't get many people here now. The hotel is not really functioning. I'm afraid I was rather unprepared." He disappeared and we signalled to the others to come in. Within minutes the old wooden table was completely full, the glasses full and the conversation flowing.

The atmosphere and the smell of the Stafelalp Hotel was exactly what I had expected Schwarzsee to be like. The walls were neglected and in need of paint. The casual appearance of the owner showed that women were not usual customers and indeed it must have surprised him to have guests descend from the mountains at such an unusual hour. A thin, dark man, he was obviously more comfortable in the presence of Herr Hausmann and the other men than the ladies of the group.

"But surely you have not run out of wine up at Schwarzsee!" he joked.

"It makes a change to be served rather than to have to serve ourselves."

The answer from Peppita seemed to satisfy him and another bottle of wine appeared on the table. The other two drinking guests leant across towards us and started to join in the conversation. One was a tall older person, who turned out to be in charge of the vast hydroelectric plant situated further along the Stafelalp Valley, and with him was a young Swiss who was his assistant there. They appeared amused and pleased at the manner in which their normal evening's drinking had been interrupted. The younger of the two stared intently in my direction and I was rather flattered by his attentions. With Gherlinda sitting beside me, her blonde hair illuminated in the soft candlelight, I rather felt at a disadvantage. I always suspected that blondes were automatically the first served.

The wine flew down my throat and romance touched the walls of the old inn that night. There was a gentleness and courtesy about the young Swiss that was different from the usual male clientele that visited Schwarzsee. Before the evening was over I had accepted an invitation to visit him one evening at the hydroelectric station itself. Certainly it sounded a novel kind of date.

The time came to return and the six of us staggered out of the hotel and stood swaying on the porch. Ahead lay an hour and a half's climb back up the mountain. The wind was cold and it was late. Our enthusiasm had gone. The pleasurable part of the evening was past and ahead was the climb home. The two Swiss wandered out with us; their way lay back downhill. The vast power complex was concealed by the trees and the dips and falls of the Alpine pastureland.

On the downward side of the Stafelalp Hotel I suddenly noticed a jeep, illuminated by the faint glimmer of light from the open doorway of the building. The two Swiss from the power station were making their way towards the jeep. The elder stopped.

"Would you like a lift some of the way back?" A universal chorus of assent greeted his question and within seconds I was squashed into the back of the jeep, which bumped in first gear along the stony paths that we had descended a few hours earlier. The great Zmutt Ridge reared up and was gone and the lights of Zermatt became visible again in the distance. The jeep ground to a halt, and we all got out.

"I'm sorry I can't take you any further. The road is not wide enough." We were standing at a fork in the Alpine path and our way lay up the steep right-hand route, but the journey had been cut by two-thirds. When I walked the route in daylight later on during my stay I could not believe that it had been possible to bring a vehicle up so high. It just shows what power alcohol has in making one attempt the impossible! Of course no one should have been driving, particularly given the narrowness of the route, the darkness, and the alcohol consumption.

As we turned to thank the driver and wave goodbye, he took me to one side.

"Don't forget. Karl hopes that you will come and visit us at the power station one night next week." He was presenting me with an order, not an invitation.

It was gone midnight by the time our heavy shoes vibrated noisily on the wooden boards of the hotel terrace. Herr Hausmann fumbled with the key and we tiptoed one by one across the stone floor of the deserted buffet and up the wooden stairway to our bedrooms. As we reached Frau Huber's office the door suddenly opened and one and all we stood aghast at the reception we might meet. She smiled benignly and lovingly.

"Come in, come in, I'm sure that you all must be very hungry after that excursion." She giggled happily at her little surprise as she presented us with slices of her favourite fruit flan. There was not one of us that dared to refuse such a well-intentioned offer, although exercise, fruit flan and wine do not mix very well, particularly after midnight, and with the start of the next working day only a few hours away.

6

It was mid-morning when I glanced out of the kitchen window in the direction of the cable car station and saw the strange sight of a silver cable car hanging motionless about fifteen yards outside the terminal. The cables were still and silent and the car moved neither downwards nor in towards its resting place.

Something had gone sadly wrong.

Together with the chef I ran over to the station to see what had happened.

There had been an accident. The cable car had approached the last pylon at too fast a speed and had crashed against it. Glass had scattered and passengers had been cut and bruised in the collision. Immediately emergency machinery had come into operation and the cable car had come to a standstill. From where I stood I could see the passengers peering unhappily from the windows, some of them looking as if they were contemplating jumping out. That, of course, was an impossibility, for the last steep rise of the cables was up the sheer face of the Schwarzsee Plateau on which I was standing and there was no way for them to descend or to be helped out.

It took nearly an hour for the cable car to be manually winched into the landing bay, foot by foot and inch by inch until it came to rest. The dishevelled and injured passengers were brought straight back to the hotel for rudimentary first aid and the necessary cups of black coffee and nips of reviving spirits. Fortunately no one was seriously hurt, and the most shaken person of all was the cable car conductor himself, a small, elderly man with a lined face like a walnut and a less friendly manner than his fellow employees.

"What happened?" was the general cry from the passengers and from the hotel staff.

"It was the wind; it was too strong," was all that he kept on saying. "It blew us against the pylon and there was nothing that I could do."

"But surely you have brought up cars in stronger winds than today's," the chef interposed. "Sometimes it is nearly gale force." The conductor only shrugged his shoulders and repeated his statement. That was what he had decided to say and to that he was going to stick. I felt sorry for him as he sat in the buffet surrounded by shouting people, a small crumpled man wishing himself a hundred

73

miles away. It was discovered later that he had in fact been driving the cable car faster than the recommended speed for the prevailing wind conditions, but the matter was never discussed again within the hotel. It was enough that no serious harm had been done.

The passengers that had come up on the ill-fated journey had to return to Furi on foot, and with them the unfortunate conductor.

I turned to Frau Huber, who had become nursing superintendent in the hour of disaster.

"How long will it take to fix the cable car?"

"Who knows? We must wait until we receive a phone call from Furi. The cars will still be running from there to Zermatt." It was fairly late in the evening when the phone message came through:

"There will be no cable cars to Schwarzsee until at least Saturday."

That was four days away.

I wondered how busy we would be in the hotel without our regular customers off-loaded every twenty minutes throughout the day. I did not have long to wonder.

The next morning we hung restlessly about the buffet and the restaurant. Hardly a dozen people were served during the course of the day, and they were the stalwarts that had decided to walk, or rather climb the steep route to the hotel from Furi. The cable car route to Schwarzsee had not been in existence when the previous hotel had functioned, and I began to think of the small amount of trade that that hotel would have done, if it had been dependent on feet rather than mechanical aids to bring clients.

By mid-afternoon the chef appeared, immaculately dressed in city suit and carrying a small suitcase.

"Where are you going, Herr Hausmann?" Frau Huber called, as he made his way towards the door. The rest of us swung curiously round in our seats to examine the smart image that stood before us.

"I'm going on holiday."

"But you can't go down the mountain dressed like that." Her eyes, and likewise all of ours, descended to his polished city shoes. His voice was gruff but determined.

"I need a holiday, so I'm taking the three days off that are owing to me now. There won't be many guests for you to cook for." His manner brooked no argument and within seconds he was gone, suitcase in hand, trousers exquisitely pressed by Peppita and as though about to catch the commuter train to London. I watched him jump and stumble down the steep path but soon he was well out of sight. I never did discover where he went on that short holiday of his. It might have been quite interesting to find out.

That evening we sat around in the hotel gazing at each other and the empty tables and suffering the noise of Frau Huber in the kitchen acting as chef.

"I wanted to ask Johann to take my shoe to be mended again."

"And I was expecting a letter. Now there will be no post arriving until the cable car is mended."

"I have a lot of money that I wanted taken to be deposited in the bank," said Frau Huber, entering in a waft of steam from the kitchen. It was now that I realized what isolation really was at Schwarzsee.

We ate in an awesome silence whilst the Italians could be heard down below in the basement relaxing and playing the radio, wondering how to amuse themselves with no washing up to be done, no vegetables to prepare for the next day, and no floors to be scrubbed clean after heavy boots had dragged in the dirt of the mountains.

Our silent munching was broken by Frau Huber.

"Maria, have you had a free day yet whilst you have been working here?"

"No."

"And Virginia, I don't think that you have had a day off yet either."

"I certainly haven't," I replied, almost too quickly.

"Then tomorrow you can both take a day off and go to Zermatt." She sat back and smiled her best beneficent smile. I was overjoyed at the prospect, and then came the punch line.

"You can both walk down together and take the money to the bank. It won't be very heavy, and then you can collect the mail from the post office on the way back when you have looked around a little."

Our smiles faded. There was a definite purpose in Frau Huber's generosity. Only mad mountain enthusiasts like Maria and myself would welcome the suggestion of a day off that warranted carrying a heavy mailbag up three thousand feet as one of its perks. We had to snatch at straws, however, and provided the weather held and we shared the task between us, some pleasure should come our way.

And so the morning of my first whole day without work dawned at Schwarzsee, and it was sunny, not a cloud in the sky. The alarm rang at 6 am and I luxuriously ignored it.

Maria was already up washing her hair for the day's adventure, and briskly preparing

a small rucksack with all that we might need. I think that she was trying to pretend that we were going mountain climbing rather than walking.

By the time we were ready to set off, the full morning was upon us, and the hotel was functioning in skeleton manner. We waved a quick farewell and in seconds vanished down the steep path behind the hotel, following in the chef's footsteps from the day before.

The sun glistened on the Monte Rosa and the Gornergletcher, which for much of the first part of the descent, were our distant companions. Above us the cables stretched endlessly, silent between the great steel pylons, and for the first time, through their silence, I became aware of the permanent whining that usually emanated from them as the cabins swung to and fro to Furi. We scattered the mountain sheep as we jumped and half ran in our haste not to waste a moment in reaching the metropolis, Zermatt village.

We had been walking for about half an hour when we heard shouting behind us and saw two young climbers following behind. They soon caught up and turned out to be two Englishmen from Manchester with whom I had talked a day or so previously.

"Where have you sprung from?"

"The Matterhorn, where else?"

"Did you manage to climb it then?"

"Just made it back to the Hörnli Hut before dark yesterday."

"Did you have a guide with you?"

"No. You wouldn't catch us paying those fees. Anyway what do we need a guide for? No more difficult than some of the Scottish rock climbs, fixed ropes on all the difficult slabs as well. We're not greenhorns, you know." I was sure they were not but I found them rather disagreeable companions as they lumbered along with Maria and I. Their dismissal of the Matterhorn annoyed my soul.

"You two got some time off then?"

"Yes."

"Your companion's a bit of a sourpuss isn't she?"

"She doesn't speak English."

Maria was indeed looking very irritated by their presence and not only irritated but worried, for in her small rucksack she was carrying about four hundred pounds of the hotel takings in ready cash. Although we had never discussed the matter before, I soon realized from Maria's face that she was the sort that would imagine the worst from our present situation, and whether robbery or rape, neither would please her. Of course, I had to admit that I did not look forward to either eventuality either, but I was prepared to trust in my fellow countrymen.

Despite their somewhat crude manners they did not appear likely robbers or rapists to me.

Soon we reached the forest section of the path and zigzagged down through the great pines at a faster rate, with Maria setting the pace. She turned to check that I was following as fast as possible. For the first time in the forest I saw the alpenrose in full bloom, glorious and red and glowing from every bank. The name is something of a misnomer, for the flower resembles small rhododendrons or azaleas. If I were a botanist of even the most meagre kind, which I am not, I probably would know that it is to this family that the alpenrose belongs. I wanted to stop and examine the alpenrose and savour its delightful appearance in the sombre undergrowth from which it grew, but Maria would brook no delay. We passed the small café at Hermettji, and soon came out into the open stretch of grassy slopes around Furi. The trees were behind us, and so also were the great snow peaks of the Monte Rosa group.

Ahead the Zermatt valley opened up and the large hotels were becoming clearly visible.

As we approached Furi I became tempted by the glistening sun-terraces of the small cafés and persuaded Maria to stop for a drink of juice to cool us after the marathon descent that we had just undertaken. Our two forced companions joined us, much to our annoyance. It was awkward because I continually had to translate to keep Maria content that they were only talking trivialities and not planning some special kind of assault.

We picked our way around the farmyard that encircled the chalet, avoiding the muddy patches near the overflowing water and hearing only the barking of an old farm dog. Within minutes we were settled on the empty terrace facing back up the way that we had come and looking at the Matterhorn, no longer the rocky dominance that we saw each day from Schwarzsee but now the unreal backdrop to every picture postcard of Zermatt.

Maria and I talked together and our companions became restless.

"Are you staying down in Zermatt tonight?" the dark, bearded one asked me quickly during a pause in our conversation.

"No, we are returning later on this afternoon."

"Why can't you stay down? I thought we might go out for a drink or something."

"I'm afraid we are expected back."

"Well couldn't you make some excuse?"

"I don't want to make any excuse, thanks." He seemed rather squashed by this reply. His desperation for female companionship after a stag holiday spent climbing in the Swiss Alps was obviously the only thing that kept him still persisting when his charms were blatantly falling on stony ground.

"I don't trust that bearded one at all, Virginia, he has very sly eyes." Said Maria in French.

Maria was nudging me and making my life very uncomfortable. After a few more desultory attempts at conversation the two Englishmen finally left us to finish our lemonades in peace and went on to Zermatt to see what else there was to see.

At last the day was ours again. We closed our eyes and just absorbed the sun, the smells of grass and the joy of being free for a few more hours.

The cable section from Furi down to Zermatt was working, but we chose to complete the descent on foot since we had plenty of time. The small path continued winding and twisting through the patchwork fields with their rudimentary wooden posts which hedged us in closely on either side. The ground was damp and slippery, but the landscape far more gently cultivated than higher up.

I was feeling a familiar ache in the back of my legs as I jolted down each steep step, when I was halted by a large obstacle blocking the path immediately in front of me. It looked like an animated hay bale stood jolting slowly of its own accord down towards the little collection of chalets and barns that lay ahead called Zum See. I moved closer to the bundle and heard a slow rhythm of breathing coming from within and as the path began to widen once again I saw an elderly woman bent almost double, dressed in black from head to foot. She was carrying the bundle on her back in a large elongated basket that was held on by straps. Maria and I slowed our pace to a crawl and tried to seem in no hurry at all, but the old woman was, in any case, unaware of our presence, all her concentration being needed to steady herself on the uneven descent.

In a resort as sophisticated as Zermatt it was surprising to see that only a mile or so from the centre of the village, life remained unchanged for the country folk, and that short skirts and professional hippies had no effect on the custom of centuries. Of course, this amazing traditionalism of the older peasant population is one of Europe's main inconsistencies. Wherever one travels, there always seems to be a grandma present that dresses and behaves as though the twentieth century is a non-event. Tall, well-dressed sons and daughters drink and dance and take advantage of the trappings of civilization, but their grandparents, particularly the womenfolk, follow behind shrunken, black and impervious to change. The woman we saw that morning above Zermatt was no exception, no more than sixty in years and yet, through years of toil to gain a living from unyielding ground, she had been worn down to the bent creature that staggered before us under her unwieldy load. As we reached the outskirts of Zum See and saw the sign to the white chapel of Santa Barbara, she turned right and disappeared into the dark recesses of an open doorway.

No sooner had we entered the hamlet of Zum See than we had passed it. The centre of Zum See was given over to a café that was empty of customers. Red check table cloths, startling in their splashes of colour, were strewn on tables that lay scattered directly on the path we were descending. Benches of uneven wooden planks were difficult to identify as separate objects from the wooden walls of the buildings against which they rested with a wobbly grace. Apart from the old woman, there was no other sign of life in the small village.

The route on from Zum See to Zermatt ran parallel to the gushing stream that finally joins the Visp, below Zermatt, and descends with its cold glacier water to the Rhone Valley twenty miles away. We crossed the water over log bridges and passed in and out of the shadows of the great trees. The path began to flatten out and was joined by the route from Zmutt and the Schonbiel Hut. The first perimeter chalets of Zermatt lay ahead. The splashing glacier waters became a proper river, dividing us from the terminal station of the Schwarzsee cable car line on the opposite bank.

We passed through the old upper village of Zermatt, the Oberdorf, with its typical high-storied wooden chalets, their balconies of geraniums flourishing in small window boxes. Gushing streams rushed and tumbled beneath their windows, forcing rocky paths in their haste to join the main river.

I now carried the rucksack with the heavy cash takings. Our main consideration was to reach the bank as soon as possible. We hurried through the square dominated by the Catholic Church on one side and Elsie's tea bar on the other and on past the spacious grounds of the Zermatterhof to the bank in the post office square. The Zermatterhof is Zermatt's largest hotel, owned by the Burgers, and a friendly rivalry exists between it and the Mont Cervin, the first-class hotel owned by the Seilers. Naturally, I knew where my particular allegiance must lie, but the the Zermatterhof's gardens and flags set well back from the main street, made it appear far more exclusive than the Mont Cervin, which lay directly on the street, only half a foot away from the crowds that parade to and fro along the main thoroughfare. The two hotels were the owners of the largest horse-drawn carriages in Zermatt and the thundering hooves of the two-horse taxis with their glittering coachmen and jingling bells were a sight to behold as I flattened myself into the nearest shop doorway to make way for the flying vehicles.

I sank gratefully into a chair in the Seilerhaus Gardens, an open air teahouse, and ordered a drink in tree-shaded luxury whilst I waited for Maria to fullfil our duties at the bank. A small quartet was playing in the forecourt of the National

Bellevue a little further down the street and a state of restful Victoriana overcame me. I sat aimlessly watching the crowds that wandered from end to end of the long village highway and listened to the faint strains of the string ensemble. I swallowed a delicious *citron pressé* at exorbitant cost. Passing in front of me were all the people that I would have been waiting on at Schwarzsee, but for the cable car accident, and sadly none of them seemed the slightest bit disconsolate at missing such a treat. Many of them looked, in fact, as though they were making their way to Gornergrat Station at the end of the village. The journey from Zermatt to the Gornergrat is the final stage of the cogwheel railway that rises from Brig. It takes tourists and skiers to one of the highest viewing points in the Alps and one of the greatest mountain panoramas outside the Himalayas. From there, at a height of over eleven thousand feet, almost parallel to the Hörnli Hut, you are within grasping distance of the Monte Rosa, the Lyscamm and the Breithorn and their glaciers. The glories of the mountain railway to the Gornergrat and the castle-style hotel that is situated at the end of the journey are well known to all visitors of Zermatt. Schwarzsee sometimes suffers as a result, since most short-term tourists to the area have time to make only one full-length excursion—the Gornergrat. For this reason I must admit that I always only grudgingly grant its splendours in conversation, since I feel a perverse sense of duty to support the less dramatic, more attainable pleasures of the little world of the Schwarzsee with its great brooding mountain monster on its doorstep. I think that without visiting Schwarzsee the Matterhorn still remains within the realm of the picturesque. Its glorious rocky dimensions cannot be properly identified without the short pilgrimage to its base plateau.

Maria was a long time in the bank and I enjoyed the chance of being alone and able to watch and think without the need for conversation. Hotel workers are almost by definition a gregarious group.

As I sat there I saw a very tall, dark-haired man walking proudly beside a gleaming pram and recognized immediately Herr Bernard Seiler, the owner and manager of the Seiler hotels in Zermatt. With him was his elegant blonde wife. They advanced up the street, the most sophisticated people visible for the entire length, nodding and smiling at workers and friends alike. If Switzerland were not so classless in its approach to the employer-employee relationship I would have said that it was almost the royal parade. They passed close to where I was sitting and I was glad to be recognized and included in their patronage. Only a few minutes later I was also spotted by Hans, the blonde joker amongst the cable car conductors. There was no such thing as a passing nod in his vocabulary, particularly where women were concerned, and within seconds he had come over to talk.

"So you are not working today."

"No, with the cable cars out of order there are few guests."

"Yes, it's peaceful for me too, but things should be back to normal within a couple of days."

"Is anything likely to happen to the conductor of the cable car that crashed?"

He shrugged. The conspiracy of fellow workers closed in. "Are you on your own?" he asked, changing the subject.

"No, I'm waiting for Maria. She's at the bank." At that moment she appeared, breathless and rushing.

"Come on you two, come and have a drink at the Pollux." We needed no second bidding and moved off towards the terrace of the Pollux Hotel, one of the favourite drinking spots of the local populace. Nobody could pass beneath the terrace without being clearly visible to all that lounged behind the wooden balustrade. It was quite convenient to be able to call out quickly and deliver a half-forgotten message to a friend who happened to pass by.

Whilst we were drinking with Hans at the Pollux, the old guide came in that I had first met after he had climbed the Breithorn with Heidi. He saw me and came over.

"Well, young lady, and have you been climbing yet?"

"I'm afraid not."

"Well, I'm not afraid to hear it. I'm very glad. It is much better to take your time and only to go when you are fully fit."

"But by then the summer may be over."

He laughed at my eagerness. "Not if you progress as well as you have done so far. I hear from Frau Huber that you climb around Schwarzsee now as though you were a sheep." From his facial expression I took this to be a sincere compliment. He then turned to Maria. "And what about you, Maria? Aren't you going to try any of our Swiss mountains?"

"I shall wait until I can have enough time to cross the Theodule Pass and see Italy," she replied.

"But the Theodule is treacherous at this time of year, there are many hidden crevasses and the melting snows make the crossing more dangerous. Surely you will not attempt it without a guide."

"I am used to the mountains."

"But you are not used to these mountains."

"A friend of mine has just completed the trip with comparative ease. He told me that conditions are not as bad as I had assumed."

"But you are a woman, my dear." For the old Swiss guide, this was the definitive argument against Maria's trip.

"Mountain climbing. Who wants anything so energetic?" Hans interposed. "Come on, let's have another drink all round."

I checked the time. It was gone three and we had yet to start our shopping spree. No more drinks, certainly. Maria dragged me past the tempting souvenir shops but I managed a quick browse around Wega's. I have never been able to resist bookshops and stationery shops and Wega's was a shop that satisfied all these likes with its fanciful stationery items, glossy postcards, gimmicky tourist take-away material and literature on Zermatt and Valais. But I managed to limit my browsing to a few minutes only and then hurry off the narrowing main street. The sun was beginning to cloud over and an ominous wisp of darkness swirled around the summit of the Matterhorn. I hoped that we should make it back to Schwarzsee before the weather broke. My clothing was not sufficient to cope with weather changes.

The gardens of the Seilerhaus tea rooms were emptying fast, and the usual motley villagers and tourists that sat on the wall of the Zermatterhof opposite the Monte Rosa hotel were now down to only a handful. We decided to take the cable car back to Furi and walk from there to save ourselves at least some of the upward journey. In the place of the heavy load of money, Maria's rucksack was now filled with fresh fruit and shampoos and my shoes that had been mended for the third time by the village cobbler. At Furi the mailbag was still waiting to be collected.

As we reached the Schwarzsee cable car station, we met a group of red-anoraked guides returning to Zermatt. I knew one of them well, for he always had with him two large Alsatian dogs—big soft creatures who loved a fuss being made of them. He told me that he was returning to Zermatt from the Hörnli Hut.

"It looks as though the weather is going to break. There won't be much climbing for the next few days. No point in staying up at the hut." The guide said. Certainly their prediction for the immediate future looked correct. By the time we arrived at Furi and set out towards the forest above, the sun was completely enveloped in a thick layer of cloud and only the lower half of the Matterhorn was still visible. The woods were very dark and the trees closed in around us. Without the patches of filtered sunlight that had illuminated the undergrowth on our journey down, the alpenroses almost vanished amidst their dark evergreen leaves. I was relieved when we hit the open ground beyond, although just as soon as we had left behind the last straggly knot of trees I felt the first drops of rain. I put on my plastic mac and watched admiringly as Maria zipped up her sensible anorak.

The path ahead rose steeply, and with heads down, we strode on, now becoming soaked to the skin in a snowstorm that had sprung from nowhere. The Monte Rosa was invisible and we did not even have the view of the hotel ahead to keep us encouraged, because the mountain immediately in front rose too steeply for us to see beyond. Small rivulets formed in the uneven path and I squelched my way upwards in saturated hush puppies, privately resolving never again to work in the mountains without adequate arctic equipment. The air became colder as we got higher and there was a sharp sting of hail in my face. There was total silence and I kept thinking of those cosy little cake shops in Zermatt that would now be packed with greedy people like myself compensating for a change in the weather by overindulgence.

Almost as suddenly as it had begun, the snowstorm abated and the sun shone through the drizzle, creating a magnificent rainbow. I slumped down onto the wet bank beside the mule path, pausing to rest my legs from the steep gradient and to admire the complete arc of light that stretched right down to the rooftops of Zermatt. I should have known better than to stop. Maria was already almost out of sight and I spent the rest of the journey back, struggling to catch up with the slim creature ahead.

At last I saw the hotel with the lights already on, for it had become quite dark. I reached the last curve of the path just in time to see Maria vanish through the open doorway. We had made it back as supper was being served. I must have appeared a most forlorn spectacle as I finally entered the dining room and found the entire staff lined up waiting for my entrance. What sympathy, I thought, how kind! But then I realized it was not me they wanted but the mailbag. Heidi rushed forward with the key to open it and within seconds I was only the outsider looking in as letters and small parcels were shared out amongst the staff, the accumulation of three days' contact with their families and homes. Almost all the staff were prolific letter writers and receivers. By the time I finally staggered into my bedroom and sank wet and messy onto the spotless white eiderdown, Maria was busy changing.

"Didn't we have a lovely time today?" she asked.

"Marvellous."

"It was so restful not to be working," she continued.

"A real rest," I repeated after her, and almost dropped asleep until I remembered that I had not eaten.

It was another two days before the cable car was fully working again. During those two days, the clouds hung heavy over Schwarzsee and the Matterhorn decided to hide from view. On the Friday night a telephone call came through.

Everything would be working normally on the following day. Almost as though by telepathy, the chef appeared late that same evening, a lonely apparition from the mountain walked through the door, and the staff was back to full strength.

Next morning the clouds rolled away, and the sun returned together with the tourists. The familiar whine of the cables sounded across the small mountain plateau and life in our tiny community returned to normal.

7

There was a small wooden building situated just below the cable car station. I had never been able to define a purpose for it until the day that I saw two mules being driven in its direction and realized that it was a stable. It was difficult to imagine what sort of jobs mules would have to undertake at Schwarzsee and for one wild moment I almost thought that the hotel was indulging in some kind of new tourist gimmick, like "Mule Rides Across the Glaciers." I only had to look out at the setting that surrounded the hotel, however, to remember that no such gimmickry was necessary to attract people to the place. Not an afternoon passed when the terrace was not crowded, and hardly a night when the bedrooms were not full with overnight guests, gazing from the balconies in suitably admiring manner. My curiosity was enough aroused by the arrival of the mule man with his animals to wander over to their stable and make a closer inspection.

A cable car had just pulled into the station and the mule man and the conductor were busy unloading boxes of supplies. In the dark shadows stood the two mules, their ears back with an anxious air, but their bodies restful and patient.

"What's going on?" I asked.

"The Belverdere is opening up for the season," was the answer I got in between large breaths from the mule man. "Is that the same as the Hörnli Hut?"

"No, it's the hotel that lies immediately behind the old hut. There's no other way of getting the supplies there except by mule." I was most curious, and watched as the inevitable crates of drinks were loaded onto the beasts of burden.

"The mules will have to be stabled here at Schwarzsee for a few days and go up and down each day until enough supplies have been delivered."

I turned to the mule man. "Are you going to stay at the hotel, then?"

He laughed. "Oh no, I shall return to Zermatt each evening. I had hoped that someone from the hotel would feed my mules each evening and change their water." It was easy to see who the volunteer was going to be, and so another job appeared added to my load. I thought how angry the little Swiss boy, Lucas, would be when he found out that such a job was going! His early evening hours were idle after the daytime guests had departed from the terrace and he could no longer hang around on the steps with a dishcloth draped over his arms, saying that he was waiting to clear the next table. I resolved immediately to give him the task of caring for the mules.

The next morning, I met the mule man having a quick coffee in the bar before his ascent up the twisting route to the ridge on which the Belvedere Hotel stood.

"Have you ever been up to the Hörnli?" he asked me.

"Not yet, but I'd like to."

"Well come up with me tomorrow morning. It's a good opportunity for you."
I was due to have another day off and was delighted to accept. So many climbers had left the Schwarzsee for the Hörnli that I felt that it was time for me too to visit the hut and see the starting point for one of the most frequented climbs in the Alps.

old Hornli Hut

That night I fed the mules with the help of Lucas, and felt almost tempted to overfeed them a little to slow their pace down the next day. The route from the hotel to the Hörnli climbed steeply to the summit of the ridge immediately overhanging the Schwarzsee plateau. I followed behind the heavily laden mules and the mule man, dressed in my thickest clothes and toughest shoes, prepared for the worst that the weather could do to me. In fact that day was gloriously sunny and before I had been climbing more than half an hour I was already feeling too hot. The pace set by the mules was fast and I soon realized that we were going to reach the Hörnli in record time. On a small wooden signpost just near the hotel it said two and a half hours to the Hörnli, but when we finally reached the hut it had taken only about half that time. When walking in Switzerland I normally found that I had to usually double their times rather than halve them. I think that the magic of my quick ascent must have been something to do with my sure-footed companions.

From the top of the first ridge the Schwarzsee Hotel appeared very small and insignificant and the mountains behind it, the Dom and the Mischabel, rose up to form a suitably grandiose backdrop. It appeared no more than a miniature bungalow set on the edge of the world. For a short spell the route ahead flattened out, and we bounced along across the last stubbly patches of grass before finally hitting the stones and the shingle. The path ahead then rose up sharply and for the next part of the journey wound its way along beneath the southern edge of the great Hörnli ridge. Nothing was visible except the rocky wall on the one side and the stony glacier bed on the other. The feet of the mules occasionally slipped, their loads shuddering ominously, but the mule man urged them on and made sure that I was following along properly in the rear.

Eventually there was nothing ahead but a great rock face, and the path narrowed considerably. He paused.

"You had better get your strength gathered together for the next bit of the climb," he warned me.

"Well I've done alright up to now, haven't I?"

"Yes." He was a man of few words. "But the next part zigzags very steeply in order to force a path up this particular bit of the route. There are forty-two bends ahead between here and the top." His hand pointed skyward as we started into the first bend, but all I could do was look down at my feet. There was no ground visible on either side of the path. On my right the view was straight down towards the northern wall of the Matterhorn and on to Stafelalp lying far below the Zmutt Ridge. On my left the Furggrat Ridge of the Matterhorn struck boldly upwards, far away across the Matterhorn glacier. I began to wish that I had as much confidence in my balance as the mules seemed to have in theirs. It was fortunate that their solid bulks were immediately in front of my nose and prevented me from knowing exactly what lay ahead at any given moment.

Up to this point we had passed no one on the journey—we had started out so early—but on this treacherous stretch we had the misfortune to come face to face with a small group of climbers on their way down. The mules with their laden packs were wider than the path and there was no room for anyone to pass us. Eventually the descending party was forced to retreat to the previous bend, where the path was at its widest, and flatten themselves against the rocks. I watched apprehensively as the front mule listed dangerously outwards as he rounded the bend, and breathed a sigh of relief as the swaying crates righted themselves and we moved off, waving a rapid farewell to a rather irritated group of tired climbers. The descent from a climb is never the most interesting part and to prolong it more than necessary can cause little but frustration.

The mule man gave a sudden whoop and hit the back mule firmly on the rump. With a kick the two mules suddenly came to a standstill right in front of the Hörnli Hut. We had arrived! I was standing at the entrance of one of the most famous old mountain huts in the Alps. It had been built in 1880 by Alexander Seiler and the Swiss Alpine Club, with the help of the Zermatt commune. It replaced the first hut that had already fallen into disuse by that date. A year or so after my visit, this hut too was replaced by a third hut on the same site. It will be a sad day for Alpine history if ever that small site should suddenly be abandoned.

The hut hardly looked large enough to cope with the great throngs of climbers that I had watched leave Schwarzsee in its direction during the course of the climbing season and, of course, it was not. The Belvedere Hotel, with its small bedrooms and dormitory accommodation, was a necessary adjunct in order to provide enough beds for those that wished to spend the night at the foot of the Hörnli Ridge. Only bona fide climbers could in fact stay in the Hörnli Hut, so that its reputation remained untarnished and its capacity not too overburdened.

The Belvedere Hotel was a rather ugly stone building with a large untidy terrace squeezed onto the small area of flat ground available, but that morning

I found the sight of the terrace most welcome. Upon arrival I saw a number of familiar faces amongst those already sitting out on its wooden benches. I quickly followed my companion past the romantic wooden hut and on to the more serviceable building. I met the young American who had married a local Swiss girl and was now operating a snowcat across the Theodule Pass, and a couple of the guides who were favourite drinkers in the Schwarzsee Hotel.

The mule man and I sank down with this group and I joined in the mirth that was going on at the time at the expense of a plimsoled American who had apparently been waiting at the Belvedere for over three days trying to persuade a guide to take him up the Matterhorn. None would accept the job, since he did not have the right equipment. He was wandering aimlessly in the entrance doorway of the hotel, slowly watching his dream evaporate before his eyes. He could not understand why plimsolls and a lightweight sweater were not enough equipment. He knew that there were fixed ropes on the difficult stretches. What was the problem?

I had only to look at the beginning of the climb just beyond the hotel, where a party was roping up for the ascent, to recognize the answer to his unspoken question. No matter how commonplace the Matterhorn climb by the Hörnli Ridge route becomes, it is still, to the inexperienced, a difficult and arduous undertaking, and to those with no knowledge of rock climbing, the strength of a guide pulling and pushing at the end of a rope is not enough to get you to the top and down again. I felt rather sorry for the young American and for his becoming an object of ridicule, but I think that my sympathy was wasted. Like a child, he was perversely determined to cling to his dream. A few days later I heard that a change in the weather and the timely end of his holiday had forced him to retreat, disconsolate and unsuccessful, to Zermatt.

Of course, the Hörnli Ridge is not the only route by which the Matterhorn can be climbed. Being a true pyramid, it has four ridges and four faces, but the Hörnli is the route that the guides refer to as the *Gewöhnlicher weg*, the "normal route." It is the route by which the Matterhorn was first successfully climbed on 14 July, 1865, by the Englishman Edward Whymper, and the route that is today both the easiest and the most popular. The story of Edward Whymper's triumph and the disaster that followed on the descent from the summit brought both him and the mountain instant fame. There is nothing like a good climbing disaster to bring a mountain everlasting popularity.

A number of factors coincided in Whymper's climb to make it a justifiably renowned climbing adventure. Edward Whymper was twenty-five years old when he managed to scale the Matterhorn and beat Jean Antoine Carrel, his Italian rival. In Whymper's successful party there were three other Englishmen and three guides, including Peter Taugwalder and his son. The party set off from the Monte Rosa Hotel with the good wishes of Alexander Seiler and the disinterest of the majority of the population of Zermatt. The party reached the summit with little difficulty. This was after years of effort and unsuccessful attempts on the part of Whymper, who had spent a lot of time in previous years convinced that the Matterhorn could more easily be scaled by the Italian ridge. In fact the Matterhorn summit was reached from the Italian side only three days after Whymper's first ascent, by Carrel, a man with whom Whymper had climbed and even discussed the possibility of a joint venture during those earlier years. Carrel, who had been born at Valtournanche, Italy, in the shadow of the Matterhorn, believed that he would be the first to reach its magnificent summit, and had been one of the first in his own valley to believe that the mountain could be climbed at all. He was forced to stand by and watch the glittering prize fall to a stranger.

The Matterhorn was one of the last great Alpine peaks to be conquered. On the descent from the summit following the *Erstbesteigung*, or "first ascent," the rope that joined the eight climbers together broke and the five that were roped below the break fell to their deaths. Only one Englishman, Whymper, survived, and with him the Taugwalders, father and son.

The bitterness and recrimination that followed the return of this trio to Zermatt has been discussed many times, and the accusations that the rope had been purposely cut by the old Taugwalder in order to preserve himself was a story that Whymper did not deny in his popular book, *Scrambles amongst the Alps*. Throughout the inquiry that followed the accident, Whymper disclaimed all responsibility. In Sir Arnold Lunn's book *Matterhorn Centenary*, perhaps for the first time since the event, there is an attempt to sort out the lies from the reality of the event itself and to make an objective analysis of the Taugwalders' part in the drama. As Sir Arnold says, Whymper's attack on the Taugwalders was unanimously rejected by the Zermatters, but their rejection remained mute, whilst Whymper's hostility was publicly displayed in his book and his various other publications. In an article in the *Alpine Journal,* Sir Arnold was the first person known to the Zermatters to publicly support the Taugwalders against Whymper. It was only after the publication of his article that the older generation of guides in the village made known their dislike of Whymper and their true feelings regarding the recriminations that had been levelled against two of their own villagers.

The broken rope rests now in Zermatt's small mountain museum, a permanent souvenir of one of the most spiteful slanders in mountain-climbing history.

In 1965 the centenary of the first climbing of the Matterhorn was celebrated by a week of festivities and I was lucky enough to be working at the Schwarzsee again. Processions and fêtes and film shows were held in the village, and tourists flocked to the Valais together with some of the generation's most famous mountaineering personalities, including Sir John Hunt representing the British Government. Also there was Luis Trenker, the Austrian climber who portrayed Carrel so sympathetically in the film *Kampf ums Matterhorn* concerning Carrel's lifelong struggle to conquer the mountain. Journalists came from all over the world; I remember having to point out which mountain was actually the Matterhorn to a philistine newsman from the *Boston Monitor*. He had flown in to Switzerland with about as much knowledge of the event as I would have of a scientific convention.

The week's activities culminated in a televised climb of the Matterhorn on 14 July 1965. The broadcast went out live throughout Europe. Christopher Brasher was there, originally intending to undertake the climb himself but prevented by an attack of piles. McNaught-Davis took his place. Unfortunately, as the great day dawned it proved to be dull and overcast and the French, Swiss, and British camera teams who had spent hours preparing in the Schwarzsee Hotel were faced with insuperable weather problems. David Dimbleby, the commentator for the British, and Manny Weber, the Swiss commentator, were hard-pushed to make the Matterhorn glow through swirling mist and overcast sky for the viewers that were watching throughout Europe.

Since the first climb, many feats of endurance and ability have been played out on the slopes of the Matterhorn, and many other famous mountaineering names have been connected with it. One of the greatest success stories was the climb by the Schmid brothers in 1931 of the north wall. When I had passed beneath this great north wall on my way to the Stafelalp Hotel, I had been struck by its forbidding appearance, for rarely does any sunlight reach its surface. Even in the height of summer, when the other faces of the Matterhorn have long since shed their winter cover, snow and ice cling to its rocks. The Matterhorn is a comparatively snow-free peak and for this reason it has always been a particularly attractive climb for English amateur enthusiasts who train on the rocks of Britain. They are, perhaps, less keen on the arduous snow and ice climbs, like that of the Monte Rosa, which involves a long snow plod before any proper climbing begins. Whatever the mountain, however, since the days of Whymper, the Englishman has found the Zermatt Valley and its ring of mountains permanently attractive. Out of the thirty-three major peaks in the valley, thirty-one were first climbed by the English.

Had the young American that I saw that morning at the Belvedere been an Englishman, he would not have bothered to wait for a guide, but would have gone on his own or with a companion and assumed that he knew enough from his own experience to cope with whatever might arise. Perhaps for his own sake it was a good thing that he was not. Hardly a climbing season passes when deaths do not occur on the Matterhorn through carelessness, lack of knowledge or preparation for such a climb, or, more often than not, changes in the weather that no advance precautions could take into account.

Whilst I worked at Schwarzsee a number of fatal accidents occurred, but in some strange way they did not greatly affect the life and workings of the hotel. There was a definite fatalism amongst the staff that made the disasters a naturally accepted part of the mountains. The climbers that stopped by on their way up, or on their way back, were all well aware of the dangers that could befall them, and if they persisted, then sympathy was a misplaced emotion should any casualty befall them.

On one occasion there had been a group of English students staying overnight in the hotel, and since I had been off-duty I had spent a very pleasant evening with them reminiscing about our home country. On the next day three of them returned to Zermatt, but the fourth went on up to the Hörnli to climb the Matterhorn on his own. He was an experienced climber and I had no fears for his safety, but on the next day word came through that there had been an accident and a lone climber had been killed. He was presumed to be English. For the first time since I had been at Schwarzsee I felt directly involved in an accident and acutely afraid. I had joked with him, and yet he was now dead. I had little knowledge of death, particularly amongst my own age group, and I was unprepared and inadequate in my reactions. Of course, I had not known him well, he was no more than a passing acquaintance, but I had known him in association with his friends and seen something of his personal life, so I knew the way that his death could affect others.

It was just before supper that I looked up from the buffet, and saw the lone English climber in the doorway, panting beneath the weight of his rucksack. I was completely speechless. I had so accepted the idea that his death was a fact that I was unable to say anything. In a morbid manner I was indulging my misery.

"Well aren't you going to ask me if I got to the top or not?" He asked, annoyed at his silent reception.

"Oh, course. Did you?" I replied.

"I did, but pretty hard going it was. Another bloke was killed yesterday you know."

"I know." I couldn't bring myself to say, "I thought it was you."

"My friends will be glad to know that it wasn't me at any rate. Have you got a phone here so that I can ring down to the village and put them out of their misery?" I pointed through the swing doors to the hallway and wandered, emotionally drained, over to the supper table. Herr Hausmann looked up at me.

"Your friend returned from the dead then, has he?" His was exactly the sort of humour I could have best done without at that particular moment.

This event ran through the back of my mind as I sat on the terrace of the Belvedere, waiting for the mule man to finish unloading his assignment before returning with me to Schwarzsee. Just beyond the end of the hotel terrace there was a rocky causeway that formed the beginning of the climb and I saw a guide having difficulty in moving his clients into the right position after roping up. I wondered how he would fare higher up when each foot must find a firm hold before moving a fraction higher. The ropes were knotted tightly round the waists of the husband and wife and they giggled nervously.

The custodian of the Hörnli Hut, Matthias Krönig, was sitting next to me and laughed at their antics. He nudged me.

"I don't hold much for their chances of doing the climb in record time. But still, at least they have been sensible enough to pick a good guide, not that all the guides from Zermatt aren't good," he quickly added, in case I should get the wrong impression.

It was both the first and the last time that I was to meet Matthias, for he died at the hut a few weeks later in the middle of a violent storm. His was a true tragedy of the mountains, but he died in the place to which he belonged.

I remember very clearly the night of his death. The first that we knew of it at the hotel was when the phone calls began to race to and fro between the village and ourselves. A few hours later I heard the sound of the cable car gliding upwards, breaking across the silence of the night. The operation was in progress to bring Matthias' body down from the Hörnli Hut. The mules were taken up and we waited patiently at the hotel, watching the lights from the small lanterns as the procession wound its way down the rocky mountain path to the hotel, with the stretcher dragging behind. It was a terrible night and Frau Huber breathed a sigh of relief when at last the burden came to rest in the hotel before continuing on by cable car to Zermatt. The danger of travelling such a route at night with such an assignment, considering the weather, was obvious. As we watched from the hotel, every disappearance of the flickering lights brought fear into our souls. There was nothing that could then be done for Matthias, but that his end should be marred by further accident and disaster was unthinkable.

The old hut did not long survive its custodian. I was glad that I had had a chance to see both before the march of change should obliterate the past, and its faithful caretakers.

My experience up on the Hörnli with the mule man had taught me one thing: I would certainly never be up to any standard suitable to climb the Matterhorn. No matter how physically fit and conditioned to high altitude I had become by my long residence at Schwarzsee, my rock-climbing experience would remain nil and my head for heights, pretty bad. One look at the great rock face that rose up in front of me as I sat that morning at the Belvedere, and the one small glimmer of hope that I had been secretly nurturing went its solitary way down the mountain. I began to cast around in the area for another mountain, hopefully a four-thousand-metre one, that was more within my level of competence.

It was a few days after this trip of mine that a young German climber came to stay at the hotel for a few days. He was an experienced Alpine climber and, in addition, had climbed widely in the Andes.

Frau Huber knew of my ambition to climb a four-thousand-metre mountain during my stay and she was always encouraging me. By the second night of the poor young German's stay at the hotel, Frau Huber had talked him into taking me on a small excursion across the Theodule Pass and up the Klein Matterhorn—a rocky outcrop that lay as a pale shadow of the Breithorn.

She approached me breathlessly as I served late on the buffet.

"Virginia, leave that for a moment. Come and meet Werner. He has said that he would be pleased to take you on his climbing expedition tomorrow."

"But Frau Huber I have no equipment, and besides you always said that I should go with a guide."

Nothing would deter her plans, and soon I was convinced to take the chance to go on a real climb with an experienced climber.

"Oh he is a very experienced young man my dear and you know it would cost you quite a few francs to go with a guide, even at the reduced rate." Frau Huber, even in the greatest excitement, was always very cost-conscious.

"Now you have nothing to worry about equipment. Maria has ample that she can loan you. You are a very lucky girl, gel." This was always her final phrase and final argument where I was concerned and I dutifully followed her through to the dining room to meet the poor young man that had been bludgeoned into dragging me up an insignificant peak and wasting a good climbing day of his short holiday. As I expected, he was a gentle creature in his mid-twenties who was totally unable to gainsay the force of Frau Huber's request. We smiled sympathetically towards each other and the most frightening experience that I have ever undertaken was set in motion.

8

I found work nothing but an intrusion upon valuable preparation time, the evening before I was due to set off on my climbing expedition with Werner.

A great deal of preparation was certainly needed to make me anything like presentable as a prospective Alpine partner. For what seemed like hours I was squeezed and zipped into other people's equipment. Most of Heidi's clothes were a fair enough fit, but there was something rather unfashionable and loose fitting about my general appearance. I had only to take a quick glance at myself in the full-length mirror on the landing to realize that I was lucky to find someone who even wished to accompany such a ragbag. Maria's tailored anorak that I had long coveted as a possible item for loan came nowhere near me when I tried to zip it up and the elegant sweaters of the two Austrian girls clung so tightly that breathing became even harder. Comfort had to come first. It was, after all, a physical endurance test that I was about to undertake, not a fashion parade. Nevertheless, I could have wished to look a little less like a large brown-and-maroon package when I was at last forced to parade in the dining room for the general criticisms and amusement of the few guests that were there that night.

I joined Werner for a coffee at his table.

"You look very sensibly equipped."

"Thank you." I supposed that was the most I could expect to hear.

"I hope you don't mind taking me with you tomorrow." I felt duty-bound under the circumstances to give him a small chance to back out.

"I am very much looking forward to having you for a companion." He smiled politely and I left it at that. The Anglo-German entente was well established. Werner was a stocky young man, little more than my own height, with a bush of untidy fair hair and deeply bronzed skin from his outdoor activities. He seemed dull but eminently safe in every respect and that, as Frau Huber told me on the side, was one of the most important factors.

"Is there anything else that I shall need?"

"Well, I can lend you an ice axe, but what about crampons?"

"I haven't been able to find any in the hotel."

"Oh well, we shall just have to make do without them; I have got ropes and flares should we need them. You had better bring along some protective cream as well. You can get very badly burned without it."

"Excuse me." Said a woman guest at the adjoining table, leaning over.

"I couldn't help overhearing you both. I think that you would be far safer to wear some type of protective mask over your face. None of the creams I have used so far were strong enough to prevent me burning." She started to delve into her pocket and finally produced a piece of gauze that was cut out with holes for eyes, nose and mouth. I held it over my face to please her, but at the ripple of laughter that spread around the dining room, I secretly decided that I would rather burn than appear so freakish. She looks, I thought, the sort of woman to wear a small paper shield over her nose the minute the sun shines into her garden, but I immediately repented my uncharitable thoughts when a moment later she also offered me the loan of a small rucksack for the excursion.

It was only after the majority of guests had left the restaurant that Werner suggested an alteration to our plans for the next day.

"I've been thinking that perhaps you would prefer to undertake a proper climb tomorrow. You see it would be very easy for us to include the Breithorn in a day trip, and then you would be able to say that you had climbed a four-thousand-metre mountain."

Of course I agreed to this change of plan. It would be so much more exciting to be climbing the beautiful Breithorn. I went to sleep for only a few hours and woke to a sky that was overcast; the few patches of blue that had appeared with the meagre sunrise had long since vanished above fairly heavy cloud.

The Gandegg Hut stands on the edge of the Theodule Glacier, on a promontory of rock that sticks out into the sea of snow and ice. From its doorway, I could see the snow trail across the glacier leading up to the Theodule Pass itself and, at its head, the Plateau Rosa, the name given to the snowfields that have turned this area into a paradise for summer skiers. The years that have passed since my first working summer at Schwarzsee have seen the full exploitation of this wild and glorious permanent snow landscape. A cable car connection from Furgg now continues to Trockener Steg, about twenty minutes' walk from the Gandegg, and a number of ski lifts stretch far across the plateau. Projected cable car extensions aim to go to the summit of the Klein Matterhorn itself, and if that were to happen the transport cable link between Italy and Switzerland at this point in the Alps would be virtually complete. For a long while there has been a cable car connection with the Plateau Rosa from the Italian side, Breuil-Cervinia—the Italian village equivalent of Zermatt. With interchange stations en route, this cable car rises from Cervinia at the head of the Valtournenche to Testa Grigia at the summit of the Theodule Pass.

Werner and I set off in the snow, plodding our way across the glacier towards the pass and the welcoming refreshment bar at the Testa Grigia terminus station. We kept our heads down, watching for the dangerous cracks that signalled the beginning of a new crevasse as the heat of the summer sun broke up the solid packs of ice. Fortunately there was a well-trodden path most of the way, and we were careful not to stray from it. It was difficult to admire the magnificent panoramas for the effort that was involved in sticking to our arduous uphill walk.

As we neared the Plateau Rosa snowfields the skiers became more numerous, and we spent most of our time avoiding tight-trousered Italian enthusiasts. Judging by the livid stripes down the sides of their ski pants and the uniform colour of their outfits, we were struggling to compete on foot with a crack team doing some strenuous summer training. They schussed and turned around us with amazing skill and speed and I felt quite dizzy and overcome with lethargy just watching, but Werner kept me moving conscientiously behind him. I thrive

on the summit of the
Breithorn in a snowstorm.

on intellectual competition from others, but when I am faced with insuperable physical odds I just back off and save myself the useless expenditure of energy. Of course, I was not competing with this team, but just watching the speed with which they covered ground in comparison to myself. The Testa Grigia cable car station was doing a good job off-loading the summer ski enthusiasts onto the eternal whitelands, and so also was the snowcat that rolled irregularly across the Theodule Pass from the Gandegg Hut bringing up skiers from the Swiss side.

Werner and I reached the restaurant of Testa Grigia at about 11 am and hung over the observation balcony, watching the active skiing scene below us. They all seemed experts—almost as soon as the Cervinia cable cars docked, the skis were clipped on and height was lost as quickly as it had been gained. The mad panic of activity made me feel that at any moment the snow in front of me might melt away and leave behind the grassy alpine meadows of a lower altitude.

There were few climbing groups around and as I looked up at the sky I realized why. The weather was definitely worsening. As though he had read my thoughts, Werner suddenly spoke.

"I think we had better be on our way, those clouds look pretty menacing. I can't see any blue sky left."

"Is it going to rain?"

"More likely, to snow, by the look of those clouds." We both looked up and felt the weight of their heaviness.

"Never mind. Let's go." He shrugged the weather off as though he had no need of its help and signalled me to follow him. At last I dared to ask.

"Is it the Breithorn then?"

"Of course!" He grinned confidently and I felt relieved. I would not have to make do with the Klein Matterhorn, a peak destined to have a cable car floating to its summit. I might just as well have waited a few years and saved the physical effort.

Whilst we had been eating our rolls and coffee at Testa Grigia I met Hanni, a young Swiss girl from the Hotel Julen. She too was off to climb the Breithorn with an Austrian companion, Karl. Neither of them were older than seventeen. They set off at the same time as Werner and myself and I could not quite decide whether they wished to follow us or join up with us. Soon we were moving rapidly across the plateau to the start of the Breithorn climb in a two-by-two crocodile. From the north side the climb is little more than a snow plod up a very steep slope, and it is considered one of the easiest climbs in the Alps to the summit of a four-thousand-metre peak. From the Zermatt side, however, and as seen from Schwarzsee, the Breithorn presents a rocky and forbidding face with only a small snowy dome at the summit. Approaching it as we were, I could now see that the snowy dome was really a continuation of the Plateau Rosa snowfields. The climb is taxing but not difficult. There is no rock climbing required, only the ability to cope with a series of steep turns amidst heavy snow.

As we approached the beginning of the first rise we passed a small climbing party, the first that we had seen. The party was making its way and was led by one of the guides that often came to Schwarzsee. Courtesies were exchanged and he recognized me.

"Where are you making for?"

"The Breithorn."

He looked perturbed.

"I've just given up the attempt for today, the weather's too unsettled." He turned to Werner, whom he recognized as the leader of what had now become a party of four, since the two teenagers stayed close to us.

"Do you know these mountains well?"

"I have a lot of climbing experience."

"Well in that case you should turn back with us."

"Oh no, I think we can make it to the top and back again in time."

"It's your decision." The guide shrugged and turned to me. "You should be going with a proper guide, you know. If I were you I should come back with me now." I hated to see the end of my excursion, and stubbornness in the face of reason made me continue with Werner.

With further words of caution the guide and his party left us, and we set off on the climb itself, roped two by two, with Werner leading. I studied his face for signs of anxiety but there were none. He still looked placid, good-natured and totally unworried. There seemed little reason for me to worry when the expert was so calm. Had I been of a suspicious nature I would have assumed that he had no concept of the possible danger that could arise from his bland confidence in his own ability as a counteracting force against bad weather conditions.

Something of the magic of the climb had gone for me, as I kept recalling the stern face of the departing guide. I began to wonder what would be happening back at the Schwarzsee Hotel and it was comforting to be able to judge almost exactly what every member of staff would be doing at that particular time of day. The discipline of hotel life was, for once, most reassuring.

There was little time for thought on the next stretch, however, all my energies being devoted to the efforts of climbing and keeping out the cold, for it had become very cold.

We had not been climbing long when it started to snow. I glanced back in the direction that we had come in, down the face of the Breithorn towards the Plateau Rosa, but nothing was visible except the puffing figures of Karl and

Hanni rising out of low cloud. The skiers had vanished and Testa Grigia was only a memory from an hour earlier.

I noticed that the two behind were speeding up and Hanni looked worried. We stopped to let them catch up, balancing at a steep angle in the deep snow.

"Are you going to carry on to the summit?" Hanni called out.

"I think so. It's not far to the top now. We might as well carry on, having come so far," Werner said.

"But how far is it? The snow is getting heavier every minute." There was a slight note of hysteria in her voice.

"Well, you can see for yourself . . ." Werner's voice trailed away as we all followed the direction of his glance upwards. There was nothing to see, only a thick blanket of snow crowding the air. The snowstorm had fully broken and the four of us were isolated in a white world.

Werner spoke again.

"I think that it would be better if we roped up as one party now. We'll make straight for the summit and then back as quickly as we can." There was no point in arguing with the expedition leader. We did as we were told, and then bent our heads against the snow, pulled the strings of the anorak hoods tight, and forced our feet upwards. It was still possible to follow the footprints that had been made by numerous climbers over the past few days of clear weather, but as the minutes ticked by they were slowly being obliterated. Soon the tracks ceased altogether.

"What now?" I called out to Werner, who was slightly ahead of me.

"Nothing. We turn back. This is the summit. Another foot or so forward and we'll be back at Schwarzsee quicker than lightening." His heavy humour left me cold. I was suffering a painful attack of anti-climax. I was on the summit in a snow blizzard.

I kept thinking of Heidi on the day that she had come back from climbing the Breithorn and how she had described the overwhelming panorama of the Alps visible from the Breithorn's summit, of Mont Blanc shining on the distant horizon and the Oberland peaks standing out clearly across the miles that separated them from Zermatt. All I could see through my frozen sunglasses was snow, and my feet felt all uncertain and awkward as I tried to turn cautiously, frightened suddenly that I might make a careless move and disappear over the unseen edge and carry the other three with me. Hanni started to cry silently, partly with vexation, partly with misery. Werner was busy rearranging the order that we should take on the rope for the descent. Karl, who had said little and done less for most of the trip, was attempting to comfort Hanni in a perfunctory manner. At his age he was obviously determined to appear entirely at ease regardless of the situation.

I was totally engrossed in trying to get my camera fixed so that Werner could take a photo of me on the summit. The camera got wet as I exposed it to the elements outside the safety of my rucksack but I did manage to get my photograph, even if it was only of my rear back view enveloped in thick mist.

The stop at the summit was short and I led the way down, this time with Werner bringing up the rear. I had gone only a short distance when I found that the tracks by which we had ascended had now completely disappeared. I was just plunging down, descending into fresh, deep snow that rose halfway up my legs at each step that I took. I slid and fell and then waited for further instruction from Werner.

"Just keep going down in short zigzag turns in the same way that we came up. We must be following roughly the same route." I tried to do as he suggested but after we had been descending in this fashion for about an hour a general uneasiness descended upon us all. The snow was definitely thickening and it was becoming very difficult to keep moving. At the same time, the steep gradient of the mountainside showed no signs of lessening. By all accounts we should have been almost nearing the Plateau Rosa and the beginning of the slow incline that would take us back towards the Theodule Pass.

"Are you sure we are going in the right direction?" I called out to Werner.

"We are going down, at any rate." His reply was too confident for my liking.

"Couldn't we take a compass bearing on our position?"

"We certainly could if I had a compass with me!" The climbing party came to a sudden halt and Hanni burst into the long-threatened sobs.

"We're lost in a snowstorm and we can't even find our way back by compass," she wailed.

"Haven't you two got a compass on you either?"

"No," replied Karl. "We thought that we shouldn't need one." I almost felt like joining Hanni in a flood of tears just to relieve my temper. Only Werner still seemed unworried.

"We must keep going. I still think that we are going in the right direction. We have probably just misjudged the time that we thought it should take us." His words were comforting and I for one was prepared to accept them, if only to stop myself worrying. Only a short time afterwards the slope did begin to lessen off and Werner's prestige rose accordingly. In between great flurries of snow it was now possible to see tens of yards ahead at intermittent intervals. We were on fairly level ground again; immediately our pace quickened and we headed back in what we thought was the direction of Testa Grigia. I remembered that on our way out, the rocky approach to the Klein Matterhorn had lain fairly close to our route. The rocks should now be showing up on our right if we were on the correct route. We all strained our eyes to see as we plodded on, attempting to penetrate the opaque blanket of snow.

"Look. Over there." Werner followed the direction of my hand and waited for the snow pall to lift momentarily.

"You're right. Over there! There are some rocks." He pulled sharply on the rope and set off almost at a run to reach the first sign of a break in the carpet of white that had been our only view for the past four or five hours. We were within a few yards of the rocks when Werner suddenly stopped.

"Get back, get back." He pushed me roughly as I almost collided into him and the other two tumbled over each other as the ropes slackened and wound around our legs.

"What's happened?" I hardly dared ask.

"Look closely. Those aren't rocks at all. That's a great crevasse right across our route." A shiver of fear went through me and for the first time I really understood the danger that we were in.

"We had better retrace our steps a little and strike off further to the west. It's impossible to say if there are any other crevasses in the area. Get back and keep the ropes at full length. Spread out and wait for me to test the ground ahead before you follow." His directions became suddenly curt as he took responsibility for our safety. What knowledge he had, he had to use, for none of us were experienced and all of us were too frightened to volunteer any suggestions of our own.

The directive to retrace our steps was a difficult one to keep, for the snow had obliterated our light footprints almost as soon as they had been made. Another halt showed that we were heading straight for an enormous, threatening crevasse that we had again assumed to be the rocky outcrop of the Klein Matterhorn. Once more we turned and as we did so, Hanni sat down in the snow.

"I can't go any further. Let's wait for the snow to stop and then we can see where we are."

"Get up at once. We must keep going. You'll freeze to death if you stay there. We must keep moving." Werner's words were firm. The damp cold was already beginning to penetrate my clothes and particularly my heavy suede climbing boots, which were not at all suited for this sort of excursion.

"I'm too tired to go on. My legs are exhausted." Hanni's wails brought only shouts from Werner. His gentle manner of the early morning was gone, and he came back to pull her roughly to her feet.

"You must keep walking. If we keep going, then we have nothing to fear. What we must do is find a way down. Sooner or later we must hit a way down. These mountains are not endless."

I felt my fingers withdrawing from my body and my stomach ached with hunger, but I tried to prevent myself from complaining. My instinct for self pres-ervation was coming to the fore and every moment's delay in dealing with the fears of Hanni seemed to me precious minutes wasted. My cry was always "Let's get on," and I found Werner's cautious testing of the ground an irritation even though I knew that it was vital. If one of us had fallen into a crevasse it would have been an impossible task to hoist the person out, for we were nearing the point of exhaustion.

I was becoming increasingly aware that the crevasses were appearing more frequently and soon we were winding our way around the great gashes in the ground rather than turning back when we came across them. The incline was becoming steeper and we were rapidly losing height. The ground was also becoming icier and I continually had to use my ice axe to prevent myself slipping.

Werner stopped again and came back to me. He unfastened one of his cram-pons and knelt down.

"Which is the foot you lead with?"

"My left."

"Ok. Then I'll strap this crampon onto your left. At least you will only slip on one foot then." I felt decidedly imbalanced as I continued with the addition of one crampon, but I was less insecure. The talons bit into the icy surface beneath the fresh covering of snow and gave me more confidence as I followed immedi-ately behind Werner. It was then that I remembered the distress flares that Wer-ner had brought and I suggested that we use them. Perhaps a search party had come out looking for us.

"No good I'm afraid. In this weather they would not penetrate even a few yards. What we need is a whistle."

Needless to say, not one of us had one.

Whilst we had been talking there had been a slight lessening in the snowfall and the clouds above became visible again. The weather had done its worst and the snowstorm was abating. We could now see quite far ahead; on all sides the snowy plateau was breaking up into a great jigsaw of ice. We had come to the head of a glacier, and one thing was certain about all glaciers—they descend to the valleys.

"This will have to be our way down. If we are cautious, we should make it. I'll jump and test the strength of the ground first. If I disappear, pull hard on the ropes. It's our only chance now."

I looked at the great formations of the ice, like icebergs in the mountains, and doubted that we should ever find a safe route down the glacier, particu-larly ill-equipped as we were, but Werner was right. The packs of ice fell away steeply in front of us, and for every foot that we lost in height we gained hopes of reaching safe ground again. The walls of ice were very high to start with, but slowly their height lessened and the crevasses became narrow enough for us to leap them. Our immediate bearings were unknown to us but we presumed that we were descending the glacier beneath the north wall of the Breithorn and that we should find our way back to the Gandegg Hut. For the first time, I began to think that our chances of survival were reasonable.

We had been walking around in the snow for six hours now, ill equipped, with no food or drink and with no bivouac equipment should we need to spend the night out of doors. It was lucky that we stumbled onto that glacier, dangerous as was the descent.

We must have been going for about another hour when the ice gave way to moraine, the shingle mass that forms the end of a glacier. My feet were squelching but the rest of my body had dried out. The snowstorm had passed and above us the clouds had lost their menacing air.

The boulders and stones made me feel as if I were walking on Brighton Beach, the rockiest and most uncomfortable beach I know, and my boots proved no protection against every jarring step. A hundred times I wished myself back at Schwarzsee, serving behind the buffet. Hanni had quietened down now that she saw a glimmer of hope and seemed prepared to accept all of Werner's instructions without further argument. For my part, I was becoming exhausted by his cheerfulness. I know that I should have been thankful for his placidity in the face of trouble, but once the end of the trouble seemed in sight his permanent even temper began to grate on my tired nerves.

For the first time since we had left Testa Grigia that morning Werner called for a rest, and the four of us sank onto a large dry boulder.and felt the remaining energy seep through our bodies. A faint air of jubilation hung over us. We had triumphed, but thanks to chance rather than to our own skills. Whilst the others were talking I was studying the valley that opened out far below us. We were still way up in the kingdom of the mountains and their glaciers, but the tree line and greenery were visible below, and over to our left, a long way further down, I thought I saw a small mountain hut. I pointed it out to my companions.

"That's the Gandegg." Hanni said.

"It isn't, Hanni, you must have passed the Gandegg on your way here this morning. It's nothing like that in position." My flat denial made us all look again. I struggled to find some recognizable landmark on the horizon that would show that we were on our way home and that Zermatt was indeed hidden in the folds of the landscape below. There was no such landmark to be seen. It was obvious that Zermatt did not lie ahead. We were not even in Switzerland.

We were in Italy. We must have turned due south in our attempts to descend from the Breithorn, instead of north. A vain hope that we might have landed up in the Valtournenche, with its easy cable car route back to Zermatt, was soon dismissed. The narrow cutting that lay ahead of us bore no relation to the view that we had looked down upon from Testa Grigia. Ahead lay an unknown Italian valley, narrow and isolated and cut off at its head by the great glaciers of the Monte Rosa massif on which we were now standing.

There was nothing to do but carry on downward and try to cut across to the hut that we could see from our lofty perch. A vague path eventually led out of the rocky base, but try as we might we never seemed able to get any nearer the hut. Soon we were walking away from it at a lower altitude in the treeline of larch and fir forests. It was nearing sunset and there was a damp scent rising up from the ground all around us. The freshly fallen snow was everywhere, making the rough pathway a constant hazard, and we slipped more than necessary because we were so tired. As I turned to look back towards the glacier I saw the clouds starting once again to roll across the summit of the Breithorn and obscure the purity of its outline. The foliage through which we were now silently walking was of a much deeper green than on the Swiss side; it had been this deep, olive colour of the trees and fields when viewed from the foot of the glacier that had first made me think that we must have crossed into Italy. The walls of the valley were high and narrow and the path became darker and more enclosed as we lost height. A small stream was running parallel to us.

At last we came across a collection of two or three chalets, dark brown and almost invisible amongst the trees in the fast-fading light. The largest amongst them had an almost illegible sign on its facade that read "Locanda."

We had found what we were looking for and, despite the fact that the place looked closed, I felt full of relief and expectation as we made our way round the side of the building to the front door. It was open. We pushed our way in and stood engulfed by the warmth and cleanliness of the little bar in which we found ourselves. A few wooden tables and chairs were scattered around and carvings hung on the whitewashed walls. There was a strong smell of Italian seasoning coming from the direction of a half-open doorway on the left. There was the sound of clattering cutlery and laughter. Obviously the owners were busy enjoying their evening meal and had long since given up the idea that any guests would materialize out of the snowstorms.

We sank into the chairs and wallowed in the comfort and attention that we received when the wife of the family discovered us, dripping wet and exhausted, in the bar. Our socks and jackets were dragged from us for drying and great tureens of minestrone were placed in front of us with hunks of bread and a large carafe of wine. There was no other food available and the husband kept apologizing for the lack of meat. He need not have bothered. I found the soup the most luxurious meal, in time and setting, that I had eaten.

The wine went to our heads after the fright and exhaustion of the day.

"Here's to ourselves."

"Cheers." We toasted ourselves in every language, to the amusement of the entire family—grandmother, parents, and children—for whom we were the focus of attention.

"Is it possible to telephone from here?"

"Oh no, I'm sorry, you will have to go on to St. Jacques for that. There is one telephone there and it is in the hotel."

"How far is the village from here, then?"

"About half an hour's walk." We all groaned.

"Where is this, then?"

"This is Fiery and high above you is the Rifugio Mezzalama. That is the hut that you must have seen. But don't worry, you can stay here tonight. We have a room with four beds in it." We were thankful for the offer, for Werner was the only person with any money on him and we certainly would not have been able to afford hotel prices for all of us. As it was, we were paying with Swiss francs and relying on the rate of exchange that we were given. Our day was not yet at an end, for we had to go on down to the village of St. Jacques to locate the one telephone and to find out how we could get back to Switzerland the next day. The agony of squeezing my feet back into my boots for the last trek was almost unbearable, for I had slight frostbite on my little toes and every small pressure hurt. The problems of making our telephone connection to the Hotel Julen in Zermatt led me to not telephone separately to Schwarzsee. Having told the management at the Julen that Hanni and Karl were safe, we asked them to phone the Hotel Schwarzsee so that Frau Huber would no longer be worried on my account.

Once the phone call had been made, a great weight seemed to have lifted. I felt much more light-headed and I let the wine take its full effect. The hotel in St. Jacques was the provider of all information in the village, and they told us of our route for the next day. According to the manager, it was possible to cross on foot to the Valtournenche from the Val D'Ayas, in which we now were, via the Col della Cime Biancho, but one look back up the steep sides of the mountain and I preferred a less scary means of getting to Cervinia.

As the crow flies we were only a few miles away, but the journey entailed three bus trips: one south down the Ayas Valley from St. Jaques to Verres, where we would change buses for Chatillon, and at Chatillon we would change again for the journey back north up to Cervinia, which lay almost exactly parallel to St. Jacques in the adjoining valley. Once we reached Cervinia we could take the cable car to Testa Grigia and from there head back on foot to Schwarzsee. There was only one bus to Verres from St. Jacques the next morning and it left at half past six.

It was early to bed that night once we had completed the steep uphill climb back to our sleeping place at Fiery at the head of the valley. The four of us were cramped into a tiny room dormitory style, but I think that we were all asleep before our heads even hit the hard, striped mattresses.

The next morning found us shattered and dishevelled in the square of St. Jacques for the start of the painful journey back. The sun was high and bright in a completely clear sky and the snow on the summit of the Breithorn gleamed tantalizingly at us. It was a perfect day for a climb, just a day too late, and we had to spend the day bouncing in local buses down one twisting and turning Alpine valley and up another. Hanni whined about the time that it took to get to Cervinia and started to fret that we would miss our cable car connection, but I was too tired and too thankful to be safe to care if we had to sit all day long waiting for our casually timed transportation. The magnificent scenery of the Valtournenche passed me by; I hardly even took a second glance at the Matterhorn from Cervinia when we eventually reached the base cable car station that would take us back to Testa Grigia. Our money, or rather Werner's money, was running out, and so were our tempers, as we continually had to beg each new bus conductor to accept our Swiss francs and to give us the right change. There was an hour's wait at Cervinia and I sat on the steps of the church in the boiling sun, grimacing up at the Italian face of the Matterhorn. From this side it lost part of its grace and beauty. It was more rugged and unkempt in appearance and the pyramid shape that so identified the Matterhorn from Zermatt was not nearly so clearly defined. The whole mountain seemed to lean. Cervinia itself was nothing but a collection of new chalets and expensively equipped modern hotels that had grown up around the old village of Breuil to cater to the influx of skiers. I longed to get back to the Swiss side and to see, once again, the silhouette of Schwarzsee, a splendidly isolated reminder of civilization.

The worst part of the journey back was the slow descent from Testa Grigia across the Theodule Pass to the Gandegg Hut with my eyes continually drawn to the Breithorn, so clear and magical and inviting in the brilliant sunshine. I cursed my chances as I watched other, more sensible climbing parties setting off towards its summit with the sure knowledge of the panorama that would be their rewarded with after a pleasant climb in perfect conditions.

At Furgg, Werner and I said goodbye to Hanni and Karl without much regret and waited for the small cable car to take us up the last steep incline to Schwarzsee plateau.

It was then, as we waited, that I realiszed that the worst part of our return home was about to come. I was suddenly roughly shaken by one of the cable car conductors whom I knew well and whom I had always considered my friend. He materialized in front of me from the Furi cable car like a fiend that has just been let out of a magic lantern.

"Virginia, how could you be so stupid? Why did you go climbing with someone so reckless? Surely you knew the dangers of these mountains. You have worried us all sick. Frau Huber has not been able to sleep all night. Where have you been? If you stayed at the Gandegg Hut why didn't you send a message?" His recriminations flowed over me as we got into the cable car for the last stage of the journey. His last sentence stuck in my mind. What did he mean? Surely the message had got through to Schwarzsee that we had wandered into Italy by mistake? Obviously something had gone sadly wrong with the communication systems between the Hotel Julen and Schwarzsee. As I stepped out of the the cable car docked at Schwarzsee, Frau Huber greeted me with shakes and kisses. They had telephoned her from the cable car station that I was on my way back. Werner stood ignored and unwanted. It was obvious that he was to be the scapegoat for the adventure.

Back at Schwarzsee I learned that no telephone message had got through the night before. Frau Huber had ordered a search party of guides to go out looking for me. It was lucky that I arrived back when I did, for the cost of paying to be rescued can be prohibitive, and rightly so. The Hotel Julen said that Hotel Schwarzsee's telephone had been out of order because of the snowstorm. That did not explain why a message had not passed through first thing the next morning when it was in full working order again.

I stayed in bed for three days afterwards with mild frostbite, exhaustion, and slight facial burns. Despite the fact that Frau Huber nursed and cosseted me like a mother, she never once let up on scolding me for the anxiety that I had caused her, the rest of the staff, and guests. Even Herr Hausmann had apparently spent the best part of the day on the balcony with binoculars, trying to locate me on the ice fields.

In comparison with Werner, however, I was lucky. Frau Huber could not forgive him at all. He was made so unwelcome that he left before I could even repay him my part of the cost of the excursion. Poor Werner! It was only his kindness that had allowed him to fall prey to such a situation in the first place.

I was glad to return to work and pull my mind from horrid nightmares of looming crevasses and thick snow. It was almost preferable to bear the teasing of my friends and the admonishing looks from Maria, whose boots I had ruined.

Maria was the last to give up scolding me because she, I soon realized, was worried more about my morals than my safety. I had spent a night with a man, and it took a lot of late-night talking in our bedroom to convince her that my total physical exhaustion that night at Fiery would have made all possible sexual dalliance a complete nonstarter, even supposing that I had felt so inclined!

9

A gang of old men arrived late one Sunday afternoon, members of a local community club in the town of Visp. They were on a group outing. About twenty in number, they tumbled unsteadily out of the cable car with never a backward glance at the magnificent scenery that surrounded them, only an onward one to the last drinking halt on the trip. Within minutes of setting foot in the clean buffet they were sprawled amongst the long wooden tables with glasses and full bottles at the ready. Their small grey moustaches quivered at the pleasure of the first sip as they settled themselves for a comfortable late-afternoon drink, and a bubble of conversation filled the hotel.

"Come on young lady, give me a kiss." The obvious leader of the group, who must have been in his late seventies, stretched up a red face towards me as I went to fill his glass, and I obliged with a quick peck on the cheek. Frau Huber must have guessed from my gesture that I had a soft spot for old men, for she called me over behind the buffet.

"Why don't you give each of them a small buttonhole as a gift before they leave?" It seemed a lovely idea to me and accordingly I set to, dismantling the bowls of alpenroses on the restaurant tables. Fortunately Maria was taking her *Zimmerstunde* at that time and was unaware of the havoc that I was causing.

I handed round the small pink posies to each guest and enjoyed the fun and laughter that accompanied the event, and the mannerisms with which some of them proceeded to fix the buttonholes into their lapels. I loved seeing their old, wrinkled faces crease with pleasure as they sat happy amongst their friends. I could have stayed all afternoon listening and attempting to appreciate their long-winded anecdotes, of which their wives and families had probably become bored years before, but their stay was only brief, for they had to catch the last cable car down to Zermatt.

The group departed more unsteadily than they had arrived, and with their departure the hotel suddenly became very empty and cold. Not even the great power of the mountains could compensate for the loss of their obvious delight in their short stay with us. I stood with Frau Huber in the doorway and waved until the last straggler had disappeared into the dark shadow of the cable car station.

"Old drunks!" It was Herr Hausmann talking, standing behind us poised to prepare the supper for the few guests that were left in the hotel that night. His customary lack of sentiment brought me back to the realities of clearing up the mess in the buffet, and as I went into the kitchen I found Maria trying to patch up the damage that I had done to her carefully arranged flower bowls.

I rapidly set about my duties with a conscientious air and tried to avoid catching Frau Huber's eye as she shot me conspiratorial glances across the buffet. I thought it best to appear as though nothing was to do with me.

A few days later another special village happening took place.

A village wedding is the sort of event that brings out the best in everyone, and the wedding that took place by the lakeside in the little chapel of Maria Zum Schnee was no exception.

A more romantic spot for a wedding it would have been difficult to create, and the fact that three-quarters of the guests had to hear the service from the porch and the grassy slopes around the lake did not in any way detract from the beauty of the event.

The reception following the wedding was held in the hotel and although it involved a greatly increased volume of work for the staff, for once no one grumbled. A wedding is very much a set piece of which each part must function perfectly, and we were all determined that our part of the event would be flawless in appearance and preparation. There was something especially exciting about organizing a wedding in such a setting, with the dreamy mountain peaks as silent witnesses and the whole village, or so it seemed, as onlookers.

The day before the wedding was to take place, Peppita, the two Austrian girls, and I spent the afternoon searching for mountain flowers with which to decorate the hotel. Since it was to be a mountain wedding, it had been decided that there should be a mountain décor. No professional bouquet could have appeared more beautiful than the great bowls of forget-me-nots, alpenroses, violets, and marguerites that we gathered from the mountain slopes under a burning hot sun.

I had been glad for the opportunity to escape the frantic preparations that were going on in the hotel itself that afternoon before the big day. Herr Hausmann was going mad in the kitchen, as seemed the correct thing to do for a chef, and the Italian couples looked all set for an especially tempestuous version of their weekly confrontation with Frau Huber.

I had spent my morning in the basement laundry passing endless white napkins through the great steam press and losing out all the time saved by the power of these great machines as corners became entangled and I ironed in more creases than I ironed out. Our journey down the mountainside to collect flowers was a far more pleasant occupation. Above us, as we bent in the long grass, the cable cars whirred more frequently than usual as they brought up extra supplies for the following day.

That night the hotel was thoroughly scrubbed and cleaned and the scent of the newly picked flowers mingled with that of polished wood. Every plate, glass, fork, and knife had a reflective shine on its surface. The success of the wedding would obviously mean a great deal to the hotel and to Frau Huber's reputation as a manager. There were not many hotels that were managed alone by a woman unless they happened to be owner-managers, and from the women's lib point of view this made it doubly important. The one thing that we could not control was the mountain weather and I just prayed that night that the Matterhorn and his neighbours would decide to stay visible, both to watch the proceedings and to be watched.

The next morning I woke up early to the most magnificent sunrise. Not a wisp of cloud blurred the outline of the Matterhorn; it was flaming with orange clarity. I crept downstairs in the silent hotel to the first floor, and unlocked an empty bedroom to let myself through onto the long veranda that ran the length of the hotel. The main meal for the wedding family and special guests was to take place on this veranda, weather permitting, and I was glad to feel the clear fresh morning coldness that usually heralded warmth later on.

Breakfast that morning was a quick event so that we could rapidly start our tasks before Frau Huber arrived to confuse us. It was inevitable that the excitement of the day ahead would bring a glorious flush to her face and trembling to her hands. The chaos that usually resulted from these symptoms would bode no good for anyone. I slunk behind the buffet with Peppita to sort the mountain of wine that was likely to be consumed. The noises coming from the kitchen immediately behind us were enough to prevent either of us satisfying any curiosity to find out what was going on in there. The saddest-faced people that morning were Gherda, Gherlinda, and Maria, the first two because they were not directly involved in the preparations, since their duties kept them upstairs in the bedrooms, and Maria because three professional waiters were being sent up from the Mont Cervin to help with the actual banquet. Maria would be unable to cope entirely alone with so many guests, despite her phenomenal efficiency, but I did not envy their reception and I watched the early arrival of the three with great interest.

By good fortune the leader of the trio was Italian.

"Buongiorno Signorina Maria, it is a pleasure to meet you." Maria thawed slightly in the face of the smooth approach of her countryman, a sleek-haired Italian in his early thirties, just beginning to run to fat.

"May I present my two colleagues, Richard who is Austrian and François who comes from—no you've guessed—France of course." The little circle standing in the kitchen laughed politely at the joke and then withdrew to a safe distance while the parlaying for position took place. I was delighted to see such interesting temporary additions to the male staff. The Casanova qualities of Herr Hausmann were noticeably lacking, and the Italian washers-up hardly classified as males at all, since it was impossible to think of them as anything but the other halves of their respective married partners. Both François and Richard were intensely handsome and very successful waiters. François was in fact a student, but I do not flatter myself that it was this mutual point of interest that made me gravitate toward his film-star good looks. I noticed before long that Heidi too found it necessary to provide them both with a great deal of information that I am sure Maria must have already given them. Nevertheless, our friendly efforts were not in vain, because before they had been there a couple of hours, Richard called me aside.

"Have you heard of the barbecue that is being held next week in Winkelmatten?"

"No."

"Well, François and I would like you and Heidi to come along if you can get away. We're organizing it for all the hotel staff in Zermatt, and it's going to be really marvellous, an all-night do, of course, because we can't start 'til late. You both ought to come you know. Ask Frau Huber if she can give you the time off." We both agreed to wait until the wedding was nearly over before asking, but we were very determined to go. At least it sounded a less dangerous outing than my previous one to the Breithorn.

That was the last chance I had that day to think about the invitation, for the wedding guests had begun to arrive and to drift into the buffet for preliminary drinks. Amongst them was the priest, whom Frau Huber quickly ushered to a quiet corner for a strong brandy to get him through the day.

At about twelve noon the wedding ceremony took place at the chapel and the hotel went completely dead. We all waited at our posts for the wedding procession, led by the newly married couple and the priest, to wind its way up the rocky path from the lake to the hotel. Lucas was the self-appointed scout. The tables were set out on the first-floor veranda, and in the restaurant for the drink-up that was to follow the main reception.

"They're coming, they're coming!" The waiters stiffened and Frau Huber flew towards the main door of the hotel that was to be used on this occasion. It was to the side of the entrance to the buffet that the guests usually passed through. The Italians crowded to the basement door, and the rest of us pressed our noses against the buffet windows. It did not seem correct to go out on the terrace. Naturally, our eyes were all on the young married couple and they were the first to be greeted by Frau Huber. They were not at all a fairy tale young couple, nor were they in any way relaxed about being the centre of attention. They appeared modest and shy and rather embarrassed by the whole affair. They were fairly alike to look at, both with short dark hair and outdoor faces, and the bride continually laughed rather nervously at all the attention she was receiving and struggled to control her long veil that the strong wind was twirling into confusion.

Elderly relatives surrounded the two. Particularly, there seemed a preponderance of old female relatives, dressed still in black, but for once with white headscarves to relieve the usual sombre covering. Guests passed straight upstairs to the feast whilst the stragglers and the less important guests tumbled directly through to the restaurant.

The feast itself was a simple one, drawing on local specialities, and was centred around a raclette party. Since being at Schwarzsee I had often heard of fondue and raclette, but had never eaten either or even seen them eaten. This was my opportunity.

The raclette was preceded by a first course consisting of a selection of charcuterie, delicately served and temptingly displayed. As fast as the plates left the kitchen they returned empty. Then it was time for the raclette, which consisted of hot melted cheese scraped onto a plate and served with jacket potatoes and gherkins. Now that may not sound a very exotic or filling meal, but no one can judge who has not tried it. The cheese starts off in a great wheel, which is slowly melted from one side only. The cheese itself has to be very carefully selected and has to be exactly the right age. For the wedding they used Val de Bagnes, a local full-fat cheese, which was not younger than two months nor older than three months, and was therefore just right for the raclette. The main goal of a raclette party is to see how many individual raclettes, or portions of cheese, you can manage to eat before either the cheese runs out or someone falls flat under the table with exhaustion. The record stands at twenty-four. Wine of course is the great accompaniment to raclette, and in the Valais, Fendant is the perfect choice. Unfortunately, the number of glasses of wine consumed tends to equal the number of raclettes eaten.

I watched from the upstairs window during a part of the wedding feast and was amazed to see that almost as soon as a portion of cheese was scraped onto a plate, a glass of wine was drained as its partner.

Fondue, the other Swiss speciality cheese dish, involves actually melting and cooking the cheese with white wine and kirsch, which sounds potentially even more alcoholic than raclette. The Swiss culinary experts assure one that by the time the fondue is ready to be eaten by dunking bread into the boiling mixture, the alcohol has evaporated, and that it is safe even for children. That is something I find difficult to believe. I have often had fondue whilst on holiday in Switzerland since my days at Schwarzsee and I have never yet managed to stand up sober from the table.

The great pleasure of a raclette party is the time that it takes, for there is nothing rushed about it, and as a wedding meal it was just right. The food and the alcohol kept apace enough to bring a happy glow and a full stomach to all the participants over a very slow period of time, and when eventually the bride and groom and their relatives were ready to move into the restaurant for the songs and speeches and general merrymaking, there was a lovely mellow air about them that allowed the staff as well as the guests to relax and enjoy the event.

Peppita and I opened the bottles of Kirsch and Williamine liqueurs that were to accompany the fresh fruit salad that rounded off the eating part of the ceremony. We settled back to enjoy the rest of the day. Things had gone well and it was not until early evening that the wedding eventually broke up in a wave of song and emotion as the newly married couple were serenaded to the start of their honeymoon on the cable car on a special late run. I dreaded to think what the swaying motion of the cable car must have done to the stomachs of some of its inmates. The day had gone without a hitch, or almost, for just before the raclette was served Frau Huber discovered that a sack of potatoes was missing and I had to do a mad dash to Furi in a specially charted cable car to locate the missing sack and make sure that we had enough potatoes should some gourmet and Swiss decide to set about beating the record number of raclettes. A possible disaster had been averted and Heidi and I were able to extract a promise from Frau Huber that we could attend the barbecue the following week.

The waiters departed without helping to clear up the debris, but that night neither did we. It was our turn to consume the remains of the feast and to finish off the open bottles of wine and to have our own small raclette party. We were making the most of a carefree evening before the hotel became fully booked during the month of August.

Frau Huber decided that singing was not enough entertainment and fetched her record player down into the restaurant for dancing. Even Herr Hausmann fell in with the spirit of things.

"Heidi, may I have the pleasure of this dance?"

"I should be honoured."

"Frau Huber, play your fastest waltz." The Swiss music blared out resonantly and the yodellers on the record struggled to keep pace with the music, as did our dancers. It had been a long time since I had even seen anyone dance a waltz, and I dreaded it when it came to my turn to dance with Herr Hausmann, who was kindly doing the rounds. I managed a few turns and then broke away into the twist. In his drunken state, the chef was not long in catching on, but I could see out of the corner of my eye that Frau Huber thoroughly disapproved of my lack of appreciation for her national music. Not long afterwards she departed to bed, taking the record player with her, and that was the signal for us to start really enjoying ourselves and to enlist the help of the only guests in the hotel that night, three Italian climbers in their middle years who had delayed their crossing of the Theodule Pass earlier that day when they realized that a wedding was to take place. We made our own music by singing, following the fashion of the wedding guests, and when the free wine ran out our Italian friends ordered more from a tired Peppita, who was still manning the bar.

It was only when I got up for work the following morning and felt the soreness of my toes that I remembered that my particular partner had danced the whole night in his climbing boots. I decided it would be singing only for me next time.

The next time was not long away, for the first of August was the Swiss National Day and once again, in the evening, Frau Huber brought down her record player, but this time we were kinder and allowed her the glory and pleasure of her public holiday. The first of August in Switzerland commemorates the day on which, in 1291, representatives of three cantonsmet at Grütli Meadow on the Vierwalstantersee and signed the Everlasting Compact. Nowadays, it is celebrated very much as the birthday of the Swiss Confederation.

The day at Schwarzsee was spent hanging bunting and flags from the lights and preparing an enormous bonfire on the slopes outside the hotel, which it was the custom to light as soon as darkness fell. On all the mountains around Zermatt similar fires were lit and there was a fair rivalry between Riffelalp and ourselves in making the flames rise higher and brighter. The celebration at Schwarzsee was very much limited to ourselves because most of the guests that were to come to us on the following day chose to stay in Zermatt for the entertainment that night and to look upwards at the fires and glowing lights of Schwarzsee from the village. For once even the Italian workers were allowed to participate, but Valentino would insist on stoking up the bonfire too soon and would almost set alight some of the spectators as the night wind caught the flames and swirled them angrily in every direction.

I had looked forward to supper on the first of August after a day of flag hanging.

"Now tonight I am going to cook supper," Frau Huber said at breakfast, "and I am going to serve a real delicacy that it is traditional to eat on our national holiday."

"What's that then, can we know in advance?" asked Maria.

"Certainly not, it is to be a surprise, but we shall all eat a little later than usual, so that we need not rush over the meal." It was a pity that she had not told us in advance, as perhaps the bravest eaters amongst us might have been able to put on a better face when she proudly advanced towards the table carrying a tray of steaming bowls of specially cooked spinach with some dreadful egg concoction sitting in the centre of the watery green mess. There is not much food that I cannot eat when the necessity arises, but I found it difficult going that night. I have asked around since about the dish but I have never again encountered anyone, even the Swiss Tourist Authorities, that will acknowledge such a dish as being traditional National Day fare. I think that Frau Huber must have been experimenting with us that night and laughing secretly that she succeeded in making us all believe her.

A more enjoyable part of the celebrations was attempting to sing the Swiss national song around the bonfire. Each of us had been presented with a small pin containing a little scroll with the words of the song printed in four languages: French, German, Italian, and Romansch, this last one being the only language of the four that Switzerland can regard as unique to itself; it is spoken in the eastern Grisons. The first verse in each language went as follows:

Cantique suisse	**Schweizerpsalm**
Sur nos monts, quand le soleil	Trittst in Morgenrot daher
Annonce un brilliant reveil,	Seh' ich dich im Strahlenmeer,
Et predit d'un plus beau jour	Dich, du Hocherhabener,
Le retour,	Herrlicher!
Les beautes de la patrie	Wenn der Alpenfirn sich rotet,
Parlent a l'ame attendrie;	Betet, freie Schweizer, betet,
Au ciel montent plus joyeux	Eure fromme Seele ahnt
Les accents d'un coeur pieux,	Gott im hehren Vaterland!
Les accents emus	Gott, den Herrn,
D'un coeur pieux.	im hehren Vaterland.

Psalm svizzer	**Salmo svizzero**
Cu la pezza bein marvegl	Quando bionda aurora
Splendurescha dil sulegl:	Il mattin, c'indora,
Cattel jeu tei adagur,	L'alma mia t'adora
Creatur!	Re del Ciel.
Scho dalunsch ils Reins ramuran,	Quando l'alpe gia rosseggia
Tier lur Diu ils Swizzers uran;	A pregare allor t'atteggia,
Leu eis Ti cun cor pattern,	In favor del patrie suol,
O Altizzim! Bab etern!	Cittadino Iddio lo vuol,
O Aktussun Babm o Bab eterbn!	Cittadino, Dio si, Dio lo vuol.

Nobody, thank goodness, attempted to sing the Romansch version!

The first of August, in addition to being the national holiday, was also momentous for being the day that Frau Huber decided that Maria and I could no longer share a bedroom together since the room was required for guests. The next day at lunch Frau Huber came out with her suggestion.

"I have been thinking that perhaps the best thing would be for you, Maria, to move into the tiny single bedroom in the hotel basement that Giovanni used to use and that you, Virginia, can share with Heidi." I just waited for the bombs to fall. The social indignity of classifying Maria as a basement Italian seemed almost a direct insult, as far as Maria was concerned. To add to that the further indignity of raising me to the peerage by allowing me to share with the secretary her large delightful room next to Frau Huber's was quite without any imagination at all.

"I'm afraid that Virginia and I do not wish to be separated. We have been working together and I refuse to go into that dreadful little room in the basement." I felt Maria's nails digging into my arms, willing agreement.

"Well we shall leave the matter for the moment and you can think it over. The only alternative would be for you both to move down to the ski cabin and that I do not think is suitable for young women." Poor Frau Huber, her last sentence had given Maria the opening that she was looking for.

"Let's go down and have a look at the ski cabin and then we can judge for ourselves whether we would prefer to move there or not." I agreed, although I must admit that I did not at all mind moving in to share with Heidi, since her room was so nice and she was much nearer my own age.

I had only been in the ski cabin a few times, when young climbers had wanted to sleep in the Matrazenlage rather than pay the expensive hotel prices. The Matrazenlage were dormitories of six or seven mattresses with blankets, rather like the arrangements in mountain climbing huts, and provided a useful, cheap form of alternative accommodation.

The old wooden stairs of the building rattled and shook as we explored the possibilities for ourselves. In addition to the dormitories, the ski cabin also contained two or three small rooms, very much in the old chalet style, with red check quilts and wooden boards that squeaked at every footfall. It was not difficult to fall in love with their rough décor and find one that was to our liking.

"I will not have Virginia sleeping down there," was Frau Huber's immediate reaction. "There are always young men sleeping in the building and there are no proper locks on any of the doors. It's not safe for a young girl.

"But surely you can trust me, Frau Huber." I said.

"And I shall personally guarantee to take care of her when we are there." Maria butted in. I felt like a child of six but had to succumb to the parental attitudes of the two of them. The idea of being outside the hotel at night had suddenly become rather appealing. The problems of entering Schwarzsee late at night if one had undertaken a mountain rendezvous with a friend were rather difficult and I had a number of invitations outstanding, which would not be early-evening affairs. The two Austrians, Gherda and Gherlinda, were wildly jealous of the opportunity that seemed to be opening up for me. The week before, Gherlinda had been invited down by one of the Italians from the village with whom she had become quite friendly and had faced the ignominious choice of staying out all night or ringing the bell at two in the morning to be greeted by an irate Frau Huber.

Maria and I eventually won the day and moved in, sticking posters on the rough wooden walls, gathering bowls of flowers, and generally making the room so pretty and homey that we became the envy of the other females. Heidi was rather sad—I think she had hoped that I would share with her and give her the opportunity to practice her near-perfect English. She did not have long to wait, however, because only a week after we had moved in, a group of very drunk German climbers stayed one night in the Matrazenlage and when they discovered that Maria and I were also there it became impossible to get to sleep. They stood outside our door, singing and calling for us to come out. As they became more drunk they rattled loudly on the door, which was only held together and locked by a small hook on the inside. Maria's hair rollers quivered with fear and temper, but I was only irritated at being unable to get to sleep. It was unfortunate that I got a not unusual desire to go to the lavatory, something that always seems to happen to me in moments of crisis, and I needed to open the door.

"I must just nip down the corridor," I whispered to Maria.

"You'll do no such thing with those men outside."

"But I must, I can't go to sleep until I have. Besides they've gone now, they have got bored with hanging around for nothing," and indeed the sound of their heavy boots falling on the floor above our heads signified that they had given up the hunt and were going to bed.

"I don't care. There may be one left outside watching. You'll just have to climb out of the window onto the flat roof and make do with that," and with no more ado she opened back the shutters and thrust me bodily out into the night, like a cat, to have my final run on the corrugated roofing.

That was enough for me. The next day I moved to the refinements of Heidi's room and Maria to her basement, and so terminated a rather pleasant partnership.

10

The evening planned for the Zermatt barbecue proved still and warm and Heidi and I delayed not a second in getting away from Schwarzsee. The slightest pause and we would have been found more work. We set off walking to Zermatt via the Zmutt route since the last cable car had already gone, and it was an evening on which it was a delight to be out of doors. The barbecue for the workers of the village was not scheduled to start until about eleven, when everyone would be at last free of their chores.

It was one of the warmest nights in the mountains, without a breath of wind, and as we crossed over the small bridge beneath Stafelalp the air hung heavy with the scent of newly scythed hay and the perfume of pine needles from the forest that lined the banks of the stream. Heidi and I ran down the stony paths in our eagerness for one of the biggest evening entertainments that had taken place in Zermatt that summer, and in addition, of course, we were very much hoping to meet up with the glamorous hosts of the event, the student waiters that had visited us on the day of the wedding.

Nightlife in Zermatt during the summer was rather limited, hence the need to organize such an event as the barbecue. The discotheques and small groups that played in most bars and small restaurants during the skiing season only functioned in the summer in a perfunctory manner, and the doors of some were permanently shut. The longer and warmer summer evenings lured people out on to the streets rather than into the little dens of smoke and music, and the climbing fraternity were a far more antisocial community, fond of early nights and early rises. For the hotel workers of the village this was a disappointment, and many a time I heard, "Oh you should come and work here in winter, then the place really swings and when you finish work there's always somewhere different to go." Coming from London, as I did, that did not sound to me all that tempting, but I must say that after living up at Schwarzsee for a few months I was quite ready for one big night out during the summer season.

When we reached the square by the church in Zermatt, there were still only a few people taking the corso in the main street; dinner was obviously being served in the large hotels. We made our way to the Pollux, where a small quartet was playing to a scattered audience. The dance floor was empty and we settled inconspicuously into a corner with a glass of beer and passed away an hour listening to a slow quickstep rhythm.

The steps of the post office in the main square, opposite the Mont Cervin. had been chosen as the meeting place for the barbeque. As we walked back up the street we found a small crowd had gathered, distributed in small groups around the square. I knew some of the faces because many had spent their free days up at Schwarzsee, but Heidi and I were outside the main circuit; we hovered on the outskirts of the group waiting for someone we knew to whom we could attach ourselves.

"So you managed to come. Well it should be very enjoyable." I swung round to find Richard, the Austrian boy, smiling down at us. "François should be along later but he has been put on late duty tonight." I was glad that he answered my unspoken question, because the barbecue would be a fiasco if François did not turn up. His good looks and attractive manner had completely won me over on the day that he had spent at Schwarzsee, and I cast a quick look around the ever-enlarging circle on the post office steps to see if there were any girls that would be likely competition for his attention.

Heidi, I could see, would be safe, for she had already been introduced by Richard to a young man from Hamburg, her home town in Germany, and they were lost in conversation. No, most of the females there seemed to be paired off, but then I realized why François and Richard had been so keen for Heidi and me to join the party. By the middle of the summer there were not many eligible young girls left in the village, and a bit of fresh blood was obviously needed at the barbecue to add a little spice to the occasion. The hotel world of Zermatt was not a particularly moral world, when a large number of young people were living and working away from families and friends within a very small community. The long working hours that many of the larger hotels exacted from their staff left romance as one of the few outlets for amusement. At Schwarzsee, in the motherly atmosphere that surrounded Frau Huber, we had been sheltered to an unexpected degree from all this, and for that reason our presence in Zermatt that night was of some interest to the males. We provided an unknown factor!

It was after eleven o'clock that evening by the time that we had all assembled and we then set off, over a hundred people, back along the high street, over the main bridge, past the Schwarzsee cable car station and out on the path to Winkelmatten. As we approached across the fields, there on a small rise ahead we could see the flames of a fire already licking the black sky. We had reached the site and drinks were beginning to flow and the music was well launched long before the stragglers at the end of the procession had reached the site.

The only light was around the bonfire and I stayed close by it, talking and dancing with a Swede and trying to avoid the popping flashes of the photographer from Perren-Barberini. It was his habit to take shots at most of the nightly events around the bars and then to post the results the next day on a board outside the shop in the main street. It was always possible to tell a successful party the night before by the speed with which people made their way down to Perren's the next morning to buy up any photographs that may lead to difficult explanations at home. It was amazing how compromising an innocent chat could look the next morning when publicly viewed in broad sunlight. I was determined to avoid seeing myself so displayed, but there was a considerable vigilance about the photographer that defeated all but the professional escapee.

"Would you like this drink?" A glass of wine was handed down to me and I looked up to find François standing there, immaculate and as attractive as I remembered him. He squatted down beside me, and whispered in my ear.

"Did you come with this Swedish fellow?"

"No, but he has been keeping me company, since both Richard and Heidi seem to have disappeared."

"Does that matter?"

"Not really, but it's just that . . ."

"Well I have come now, so you don't need to talk to the Swede any more. Let's go and have a drink over there where it is a little quieter," and darker, he could have added, as I stumbled along behind him to a small patch of grass on the opposite side of the hill. The manner in which he assumed that I had been waiting only for him rather grated, but then I supposed it was better than being ignored. I shivered as a small breeze began to get up and his arm slid round my shoulder and he used it as a useful excuse to move closer. I began to wish that Heidi was at least visible somewhere.

"I think perhaps that I should see where my friend has gone. She may be looking for me."

Francois laughed. "What do you want to find her for when you work together each day? You have me to talk to now. Let's go for a walk."

"I'd rather not."

"I'd rather not." He mimicked my English accent and suddenly ran down the slope of the small hill, pulling me after him, and I slipped and fell. It was exactly what he wanted. I quickly realized that I had bitten off more than I could chew. He had obviously been drinking fairly heavily and had also grossly overestimated my intentions in coming to the barbecue. I started to fight him off and to call out for help, but we had gone a fair distance from the main group and my voice was just lost in the darkness that surrounded me. Two shadows suddenly became visible walking along the rough pathway towards us.

"It is them." It was Richard's voice. "What on earth's happening?"

"What the hell did you want to invite those two down from Schwarzsee for? They haven't caught the spirit of this at all." François was spitting out his words, furious with me, and angry at being caught looking so stupid by his friend.

"You are an idiot François, can't you tell what type of girl you are dealing with? You've been drinking too much, that's your trouble. Come on Virginia, come back with us and join the rest of the party. Things are beginning to break up now anyway."

I set off immediately with Richard and his friend, the boy from Hamburg, and soon rejoined Heidi. François scowled on the fringe of the group around the bonfire, and his thick dark hair and shining black eyes suddenly appeared quite unattractive to me. He mumbled to himself and pottered off to fall in a drunken sleep amongst the bushes, and that was the last time I ever saw him.

The problem that now faced Heidi and me was, where were we to spend the night? Most of the people who had been at the barbecue had returned to the village as soon as the drink ran out, which was not long because of the large numbers of gatecrashers, and the all-night party that we had been promised had evaporated. Our only beds, or at least the only ones that Heidi and I wished to sleep in, were back at Schwarzsee, and the next cable car did not leave until seven in the morning.

"I suppose we could keep the fire going and stay talking most of the night," suggested Heidi amidst a great yawn.

"Impossible."

"We could go down and sleep in that old hay barn. At least we could be sheltered and dry, and it should be fairly clean inside." Richard's suggestion was eagerly adopted and the six of us who were left clambered down towards the small chalet that was nestled in the trees near the site of the barbecue. We climbed up the old wooden ladder and tumbled to sleep just as the first streaks of dawn were beginning to appear in the sky. We did not even notice the earthy smells of our surroundings.

As I awoke to the sunrise a few hours later, feeling dishevelled and dirty, there was a strong feeling of anticlimax hanging in the air, and it was a wan pair indeed that returned to Schwarzsee on the early-morning cable car ready to start work after the grand and glorious night in Zermatt. The jealousy of Gherda and Gherlinda at having missed the event was somewhat tempered by our appearance. Maria could only look satisfied that she had proved correct in her admonitions as to what the affair would be like. Unfortunately it was not to end there, for two days later Heidi and I were called into the office by an irate Frau Huber.

"The police have just telephoned. You have both to go down to the police station this afternoon. It is about the barbecue."

"What on earth happened? Why do they want to see us?"

"It seems that residents in the village complained about the noise, which could be heard two miles away, and in addition no bonfires should have been lit amongst the trees because of the fire risk."

"But that was nothing to do with us. We didn't organize the event. We were only invited down as guests."

"Oh I know that well enough, but unfortunately your so-called friends gave your names in the list of those present, saying that you were amongst the few that they could remember by name. It's not very good publicity for the hotel you know." Heidi and I stole a glance at each other but refrained from saying anything in front of Frau Huber. It was clear that we had been used as scapegoats, following the mess with François. Well, it certainly taught us a lesson, and I must say that the trip to the police station for a reprimand from a rather embarrassed policeman did serve the useful purpose of enabling us to hurry along to the photographers' to buy up the last shreds of evidence that we had ever attended such an event.

At Schwarzsee, under the watchful eye of our elders and betters, mild flirtations were much safer and more in order. The preponderance of males amongst the guests and females amongst the staff meant that the normal relationship of worker and visitor did not apply, so that the necessity of journeying to Zermatt to find a bit of excitement and adventure was really unnecessary.

It was mainly the Italian guests that proved to be the most entertaining. They were overtly the most dangerous because of their automatic desire to be considered immediately attractive and their equal desire to make every female on the staff feel that she was the most desirable person there. First came the great flattery, then the slow response, then followed the invitation, followed by the quick refusal, and last came the pleasant evening conversations and sing-song over a glass of wine with no hard feelings all around.

With the English mountaineers that came there was for me the comradeship of fellow countrymen meeting abroad in a rather strange situation and the obvious desire to talk and discover everything before one parted. I remember a particular student that wandered into the hotel and immediately struck up an animated conversation with me once he discovered that I too was English.

Within minutes I had given him my London address, and it was in the dark months of the following winter when I was back in London, with Schwarzsee a wonderful dream, that I received a telephone call from the same student. He invited me to dinner, and having nothing better to do on the particular evening, I accepted, full of misgivings, since I could recall nothing but his name. The evening was bad from the moment that I first walked straight past him standing beside the waiting taxi.

"Hello Virginia, you do remember me don't you?"

"Why of course," I lied, "It's just that I didn't recognize you for a moment without your suntan." It was an attempt, and that was how the evening went. Without the magic of the mountain setting to exclaim at during the pauses when the conversation dried up, we were left with nothing but the "do-you-remember" routine, which after one afternoon was a pretty short one. No wonder most holiday romances remain just that.

Of all the guests that I would have enjoyed an evening with in London at a future date, none would have been better than a Swiss man who stayed at Schwarzsee for three weeks by the name of Otto Muller. He was in his midforties, fat, unattractive, fluent in English and Italian as well as French and German, and a man totally uninterested in mountains and the natural surroundings of the hotel. From the first it seemed strange that such a man, with his feet permanently in bedroom slippers because of corns, should wish to holiday in such obviously unsuitable surroundings. He was highly intelligent and wealthy, however, so nobody questioned his decision. After two weeks on his own, he was joined by a rather frumpish wife from Zurich along with his elderly mother, who had considerable difficulty breathing at such an altitude. One could only assume that he wished to kill her off by subjecting her to such rigours. Apart from all this he was, I found, one of the most entertaining conversationalists that I had met, and I was completely impressed by him and his tales of the London School of Economics, where he had spent a year. As a prospective student of London University, I was avid for all the crumbs of information that he could provide. He was so much older than me and yet always treated me as an equal. I was exceptionally flattered and influenced by what he told me. I must admit that his wife was equally pleasant to me and took me with her on many a short excursion whilst her husband waved us off from the terrace, with his sore toes firmly cushioned against walking on anything other than dry planks. When he left he presented me with a handsome tip, and I often thought about him with interest and kindness when I was at college, for he certainly had been a very kind man to me.

I went back to Schwarzsee the following summer and, during the course of reminiscence, I asked after Herr Muller. A very heavy silence fell upon the assembled group and Frau Huber shook her head sadly. I thought that perhaps some dreadful accident had befallen him.

"No my dear, nothing like that I'm afraid. You will never guess but Herr Muller was a criminal. He defrauded the Swiss government of over a million francs. He was hiding here you know last summer, but now poor man, he is having to pay the price." Poor Herr Muller indeed, but then no doubt a man of his obvious talents would find prison quite a fertile germinating ground for future schemes.

The only other Swiss with whom I became at all friendly was the young man, from the hydroelectric station down below Stafelalp who had invited me for a visit. It was a long time before I decided to take up the invitation, since the difficulties of getting an evening off as the season reached its peak became more and more overwhelming. He rang me several times, and eventually when Frau Huber was within earshot.

"Why, of course you can go, my dear. He is a very nice young man and will give you a very pleasant evening."

Karl agreed to meet me at the Schwarzsee chapel and from there, escort me back to his place of work.

It was awesome approaching the vast electricity complex in the evening twilight. The thunderous roar of the machines knocked all sense from my head and the garish illuminations blinded me after the darkness of the deserted mountainside down which we had just climbed. The size of the building close to made even the Matterhorn diminish in proportion, and the sheer magnitude of machinery in the empty valley path was eerie and frightening. I was glad when Karl led me round to the private apartments where he stayed with the manager of the works. After explaining some of the complexities of the plant to me, the two of them entertained me with a meal they cooked themselves and with a projector show of slides of their various holidays abroad. It was a delightful and ingenuous manner in which they looked after me that evening in their bachelor pad buried within a barrage of floodlit metal, and I hardly noticed the discomfort of the jeep ride back towards Schwarzsee, when the vehicle seemed to slip and slide along the very edge of each precipice.

It was the start of a pleasant friendship, and Karl and I often walked the slopes around the hotel in the evening, talking and admiring the landscape, the old chapel by the lake often lending its porch as our meeting place when the grind of work was done. There was no great romance, no sadness on either side when I left. It was just that a pleasant number of summer evenings had been passed without complication and that two people, in their isolated jobs, each provided the other with some extra interest beyond the narrow environments in which they were bound for a short term of work. It was good for me to be able to get away, if only for an hour, from the faces with which I lived and worked and ate through the twenty-four hours of each day.

By September the nights became colder, however, and the walks less frequent. As the hotel emptied of its overnight guests and work became lighter Karl came into the hotel and drank with the rest of us and some of the magic of the solitary mountain conversations was lost.

It was at about this time that an end-of-season demise came upon the hotel as everything geared towards its closure prior to the skiing season. I was scheduled to leave before the actual closure and I was glad that my last evening looking out on the Matterhorn from my bedroom window was spent whilst the hotel was still occupied. Its own time machine restlessly moved to service the customers who were still pouring out of the cable car when I took my last ride down to Zermatt and to the train that would take me back to civilization and away from the mountains that I had grown to love as intimate neighbours and companions. There was little time for sad farewells, for our lives were still only secondary in importance to the needs of the guests, and I was glad to slip away quickly with just a wave and a backward glance at the hotel. As I descended in the cable car it looked perched like a primitive rock laid out at the base of its great protector, the Matterhorn.

EPILOGUE ONE, 1983

The pain of nostalgia is strong, especially today when rapid change has overcome places one has known and loved and turned them into concrete jungles almost overnight.

Zermatt, fortunately, has not yet been fully exploited and transformed into a resort where no mountains are visible for the modern buildings. The only reason for this is its location. No matter how high the chalets creep above the village and into the forests, the terrain that guards the lower fortresses of the great Alpine peaks ringing the Zermatt Valley can never be made hospitable to the permanent resident. It is a world left mainly for the adventurer and the sportsman, not for the speculator and property developer.

But if the mountains remain as yet defended, Zermatt itself is hardly recognizable as the small community into which I first stepped eleven years ago, overwhelmed by its beauty and marvelling at everything I saw. Chalets have proliferated on the slope and byway leading from the main street. I cannot reasonably bemoan its growth, since I would have been one of the very people that would have loved to live in Zermatt, and that would have demanded a choice of suitable accommodation.

At present Zermatt can accommodate almost thirteen thousand visitors, an increase of enormous proportions over the last ten years, and it is estimated that within the next decade this figure will be pushed up to forty thousand. I find it difficult to contemplate such an increase. At the moment most new buildings within the village have kept very much to the chalet style and within the existing historical sentiment. If the village is to expand, as the forecasts suggest, then I can only shudder at the thought of the vast modern complexes that must be built to provide for fresh hordes.

Already, buildings have been standing long enough for the demolition men to have found jobs, and the new is beginning to replace the old. I always loved the grandeur of the Hotel Victoria, situated as it was immediately facing the station square. Its Victorian opulence was a classic example of the hotels that were built in Switzerland during the nineteenth century, when English tourists first flocked to the mountains. Now it has gone, and in its place an ugly modern building has risen, full of amenities and, one presumes, full of financial rewards for its owners, the Seilers. The Seilers own both the old and the new, and I suppose they can afford more than most to dispense with a little history when only a little further up the road still stands the Monte Rosa Hotel.

Possibly what has saved Zermatt longer than some of its rival resorts from total commercialization is its relative inaccessibility. In the age of car travel it is still not possible for tourists to reach Zermatt by car. Up to a few years ago, cars could only go as far as St. Niklaus. This was then extended to Randa further up the valley, and finally in 1971 visitors to Zermatt could drive as far as Tasch, the last village before you reach Zermatt itself.

It looked as though the end was in sight for Zermatt—and indeed residents of the village can drive right through with special permits—but the same does not apply to tourists. Fortunately, the expense of building a road to cope with the projected volume of traffic over the last stretch of ground was prohibitive because of technical difficulties, and the plan had to be shelved. It is over this last stretch that the problems arose, because any road that was built would lie directly in the main avalanche path. Whereas the railway is protected from such dangers by its galleries, the equivalent protection for a road today would prove prohibitively expensive.

A second factor that has kept the masses away from the Zermatt Valley is the special effort required to reach Zermatt. It does not lend itself to the European tour with stopovers in five centres, situated as it is at the furthest end of a long and narrow valley. There is still an element of a pilgrimage necessary if one wants to get there, and it is the small red train glinting in the sunlight that must carry the bulk of the visitors to their destination. It is the mass excitement generated by that panoramic train journey from the valley floor of the Rhone up to the great giants of snow and ice that keeps the mystique of visiting Zermatt still alive for so many. Whenever I have returned to Zermatt and Schwarzsee, whether in summer or winter, the excitement of waiting for that small train to swing on its tracks and prepare for the rapid rise up the Visptal has never diminished. Even writing now, I can smell the fields and hedgerows of the slowly passing countryside and feel the ever-cooling air as one gains altitude and the light breeze blows through the wooden compartments.

The last time that I took the journey from Zermatt by cable car and returned to the Schwarzsee itself, I feared being disappointed by my first view of the hotel and the little plateau that I had considered my own preserve for those few months. When I reached Furi, I found that I must use the Furgg cable car link to Schwarzsee rather than take the old more spectacular route that mounted so suddenly up over the last rocky wall of the plateau. Apparently that route was now only used in the height of the season and particularly during the winter months when skiers flock to the hotel during the daylight hours. It was less impressive to approach Schwarzsee by what I consider the back door, for the route to Schwarzsee from Furgg creeps up gently and arrives right on the door-step of the hotel. But I was not disappointed when I finally crossed the terrace and stepped into the crowded lunchtime buffet.

Once again, I was immediately absorbed into the casual world of the hotel's clientele. Some things had changed, for there was now a covered entrance from the buffet doorway, and behind the buffet no longer stood Frau Huber, who had retired a year or two earlier. Now there was the new Austrian manager and his wife. I sank into a corner by the window nearest to the Matterhorn and looked out on to that glorious peak. I regained my familiarity with every detail of its classic outline and renewed my love affair with Schwarzsee and its little kingdom.

Behind me, I could hear the noise and laughter of the lunchtime ritual and the usual crowd of workers chatting to the young girl behind the buffet. A few faces I recognized, but I chose to stay unremembered. As a worker I had been immediately accepted. As a guest, a married woman, now, with my own daugh-ter, it would have been difficult to reestablish anything of that past easy friend-ship. I was just one amongst hundreds that made the trip to Schwarzsee that summer, and as a tourist I was an outsider looking in.

I wandered down to the lake and climbed, rather breathlessly I must admit, for I was out of practice, up to the small ridge of the Hörnli outcrop, and looked down upon Schwarzsee, with the village of Zermatt nestling below it in dark shadows. From that vantage point nothing had changed, the great mountain panorama taking over and bringing a sense of timelessness to the scene that lay before me. Within the hotel, I could still have thought to find Frau Huber and Maria and Heidi and the Italians, but I was only deceiving myself.

EPILOGUE TWO, 2014

I am ready to make my pilgrimage back to the place that allowed me to grow up in peace and safety in an international community.

If you want to know what Schwarzsee Hotel looks like now, I suggest you Google its name and the word Zermatt. Astonishingly, you will find a Hotel that looks totally unchanged, standing against its mountain backdrop, beautiful as ever. Even better, read the reviews, and hear the same sort of superlative comments that appear in this book. How wonderful is that.

I am ready to go. Come with me.